HOW TO SELL ON AMAZON FOR BEGINNERS

EVERYTHING YOU NEED TO SELL ON AMAZON FBA

**MONEY MAKER
PUBLISHING**

CONTENTS

INTRODUCTION

One of the best things about Amazon FBA is that it doesn't require an especially large set of technical skills. The skills you will need are not extremely difficult to begin learning, and once you see your first tastes of success, it will become easier to continue pushing forward into new product territory. Of course, there is going to be investments in time and money involved, but even the smallest investments can start the process off right. This is not a get rich quick scheme, so making careful decisions is of the utmost importance. Still, all investment involves some amount of risk, and at some point, you have to make a confident decision even if there's no guarantee that it will pay off.

When looking into ecommerce as a means to control your own financial freedom and earn your living, it is an obvious necessity to consider Amazon as part of your process. Even if your intention is to grow outside of Amazon, ignoring this market is foolhardy at best. Indeed, there are plenty of entrepreneurs that are using Amazon's Fulfillment by Amazon exclusively in order to build their online business and secure their financial freedom.

It is essentially a way for you to sell products online and to gain profits from it. Like any business, it requires the right set of knowledge and skills. Furthermore, it requires you to make decisions on the fly. We will teach you all of that and more once you start to get your knowledge up to par.

This book is geared towards people who are just starting out their Amazon FBA business; however, there are also some amazing techniques in this book that you could use to grow your already advanced business. We will show you how to get more sales with Amazon, and how to market your product the right way.

It is very important that you understand this concept as it will help you to grow your business tremendously. We will be covering some amazing topics, so hang tight and keep on reading. One more thing; if you don't understand some concepts, then we would advise you to take your time and come back to the subject. Make sure you fully understand the knowledge in this book before you move on.

To thank you for your purchase, we're offering the guide *How to Use Digital Ads to Grow Your Sales and Revenues* exclusively for the readers of *How to Sell on Amazon for Beginners.*

By downloading this pdf you will learn how to use digital ads to sell more and more!

Click here to access your free gift or scan the QR code.

1. THE POWER OF ONLINE BUSINESS

There are so much information that you can find related to this mysterious title called AMAZON FBA, and yes you might heard some people making tons of money and living a good life, some refer to as a laptop lifestyle, still have to get down some ground work in order to get there, so you have to know exactly where to start.

What you really should do, no matter you have the money and time to invest right now, and you want to skip all the fluff, there is something really important you must have right from the beginning before start to invest in any Business, and that's indeed the Mindset!

First you might see people looking at you strangely and asking you questions about certain topics that even experienced Business owners would have a hard time to answer, and most of these people will try to talk you out of it faster than you think.

Now again, in order to be successful you must visualize your future, set goals, make sure you understand your current situation, as well where you want to be within what time frame, and you have to see yourself that you are on your way already.

Mindset is so important, that if you don't have it right at the beginning, there are multiple possibilities of failures such as: that you might just read about the topic and won't take any action, stop at half way, and blame something or someone, or you might carry on but will fail in Business.

However once you have the Mindset then you realize that anything is achievable, even if you fail in your first Online Business, you will not look at this as a failure, rather just another step to your goal, learn from it, and move on.

When failure happens, and tell your friends or family about a little problem or issue that you are facing, they will think that you have failed forever, and will keep on hearing noise like:

To be successful either offline or Online you must have a mindset that any failure you might encounter it's a simply another step to reach your goal.

Indeed it's so powerful that once you get this right, some people might stop talking to you, as you will believe in yourself so much that people around you will think that you have gone crazy, you will sound different, more confident in yourself, eventually you will not only believe, but you will know that you can achieve something that you have never accomplished before.

Once you have this right, you will treat Online Business, or any Business in this matter very seriously, and you will quickly realize that you will adopt a completely new yet not known attitude that will empower you to attain great results.

Results are indeed that differentiate people, and they will truly make you proud, and they can be reached only once you start taking action on your existing knowledge.

Do not intent to be perfect, as nothing and no one is, however once you have accomplished your first result, you will then have an opportunity to do your additional modification, perhaps upgrades and then can start enjoying even better results.

When it comes to a Business idea, most of us thinking and intending to make money of it and become rich overnight.

Some of us fail to recognize there is a really hard work and possibly multiple failure took place before most of these huge success stories.

You might be also familiar with the term Passive Income! Now again, in order to achieve passive Income in life, there are lots of active work involved at least at the beginning, also must do maintenance frequently, in any cases even we talk about software or physical products, and not even mentioning that the Market trends are always in change.

Some things are might be very profitable products and goes very well all year around, however in few years down the road, will disappear, and won't be favor to anyone anymore.

Not trying to explain that there is no Passive Income, but as you see, due to continuous maintenance involved, there is some active work required as well.

To achieve so called Passive Income, you truly need to outsource all task that participate of your Business.

When it comes to modelling a Business, some of us still like the idea of running something based on a physical location, that is well decorated, clear lights with shop name and being on site, expecting Customers walking in and out, who we can serve, or help them out, and these are great ideas.

When it comes to Online Business, there is nothing easier then start selling on Amazon, preferably taking advantages of Amazon FBA.

Off course there is nothing wrong with creating a brand-new website, and start selling products, however, there are multiple variables that needs to be understood regards to large platform like Amazon, Shopify, Etsy, e-Bay etc…

Again creating your own website, having a payment platform, can be time consuming, and even once it's up and running, must be advertised and Google search engine will not take every websites straight to the first page simply because there is to traffic generated yet, even it's the best Website ever.

In order to understand search engine optimization aka SEO, and Google algorithm it's a whole other topic, and this book strictly focusing on AMAZON FBA, and now will elaborate on why began to learn about AMAZON would be a wise choice.

2. UNDERSTAND AMAZON FBA

W hat does the FBA stand for? It stands for Fulfillment by Amazon. Think of Amazon as similar to Shopify, except for two things. Firstly, you will be selling your products on Amazon, and secondly, you will have to ship your products to their warehouse before you can start fulfilling orders. So, you will have to find a supplier and ship the products to the nearest Amazon warehouse. The upfront investment would be a little bit higher when compared to Shopify. To break it down, here is the approximate cost of startup.

Buying products in bulk for cheap - $1000 - $3,000

If you sell more than 40+ items a month, you will have to pay $39.99

On the lower end, you can get started for USD 1,000 to USD 3,000 plus $39.99 a month if you sell more than 40 products. There is also a charge per shipped product, but that will be decided based on your payout.

So, even though there is a significant upfront investment, there are still a lot of advantages. For instance, you will be promoting your product on a website which already gets a bunch of free traffic. This means you will have more success in the beginning while sell your products when compared to other methods. You also don't have to worry about creating a storefront as Amazon would be your storefront.

So, without further ado, let's get into the specifics of starting your business from the ground up using Amazon FBA. Mostly, you will have to figure out three things before you begin to advertise on this platform:

- Profitable Products
- Finding a supplier
- Advertising your product
- Profitable Product

HOW MUCH MONEY CAN YOU MAKE?

So, of course, everyone wants to know how much money they can make. Well, to begin with, I would like to say a lot! Yes, you can make a lot of money with this business model. But there is a catch; if you want to make loads of money, this business can't be passive in the beginning. There will be a lot of trial and error before you can make this business passive. Now the good part is that once you get the ball rolling, it takes little to no effort to upkeep the company. So, if you follow everything written in this book correctly, you can make anywhere from $1,000 to $100,000.

In order to get started with Amazon FBA, you just have sign up and start sending your products to them. They have a highly structured store house to store your inventory, and pack them and ships them to the place of delivery when required. Amazon also provides customer service.

HOW DOES FBA WORK?

Your products become eligible for free shipping if they are priced at $35 or above. Free delivery options are for your products listed on Amazon.com. You can sell your products at a competitive price and hence get them delivered for free. The products are delivered with an FBA logo, which assures customers that the product is packaged and delivered by Amazon.

A very interesting thing about FBA is that you can take orders using other sales channels and ask FBA to return your inventory anytime. You can manage your inventory stored at Amazon through an online user interface.

A few steps are listed below for using FBA:

Step 1: Send the inventory to Amazon

- You have to send your products to the fulfillment center of Amazon.com.
- Upload your itemized list to the Seller Central.
- Let Amazon fulfill your inventory in part or in full.
- Get the PDF labels printed that are provided by Amazon.
- Use discounted shipping provided by Amazon. You can list a carrier on your own as well.

Step 2: Amazon will store your products

- When Amazon receives your products, they are scanned before storing.
- Amazon uses unit dimensions required for storage.
- You can monitor your inventory through a unified tracking system.

Step 3: Orders are placed by the customers

- Amazon will fulfill the orders for products listed on Amazon or you can submit for sales not listed on their website.
- Your product listings are ranked pricewise, since they are eligible for free delivery if priced above $35.
- Prime* members of Amazon can upgrade the options for shipping for listing to be eligible for FBA. (Prime: It excludes fulfillment orders from more than one channel ordered from different services and websites, which include Checkout by Amazon and Amazon Webstore.)

Step 4: The orders are picked and packed by Amazon.

- The FBA picks the ordered products from the inventory. They are suitably packed for delivery.
- Customers have the option to combine other orders with your orders fulfilled by Amazon.

Step 5: Your products are shipped

- Using the network of fulfillment outlets, your products are shipped to the customers by the method they have chosen.
- Tracking information is provided by Amazon for customers.
- Customer service is also provided by Amazon after sales take place.

WHAT TO SELL ON AMAZON?

As a beginner, it's always good to learn the secrets of a platform and gain an understanding of what it can offer you before buying costly stock and tools. Starting small and discovering a business from the ground up allows you to get acquainted with every step of the process of selling on Amazon, teaching you what the marketplace is all about. This will help you manage your downtime and recognize your shortcomings. You need to know the marketplace well in order to see if there is anything about Amazon that doesn't work for you and whether there are any issues that should be addressed at an early stage. This approach helps you understand the ins and outs of selling through Amazon FBA. Eventually, you will see that that are many markets that can generate income for you, with the help of FBA.

As a new seller, consider selling unwanted media items (such as CDs, video games) from your house for your first Amazon sale. This is the best way to find out the nuances of doing business on Amazon without having to deal with any serious implications/dangerous purchasing decisions. You need to discover ways of generating profit margins on the Amazon platform by selling items that can earn a 100 percent. For example, if you have a book that you have already read, you have already gotten your money's worth. Consider selling it on Amazon, as any money made from it is actually 100 percent profit.

Besides looking at what's lying around your house, you can also ask your relatives, family members, friends or neighbors if they want to contribute items to help you do business with Amazon. Consider how the world of technology is altering the way people shop and save their media. The world is going digital, and this fact can be used to your benefit. Consider what is compatible with today's e-world and assess whether any items you have will add value to the type of media people collect today. Don't be deterred because something seems "old fashioned." There's a market for most things including magazines, books, CDs, etc. Scour your house, and don't forget the attic and garage.

The bottom line is to start discovering items to sell—even if it's just a "useless" product which has been lying unused in your basement for months. To know the real worth of your items, study Amazon's marketplace. As you discover the real value of your items on the platform, you will be able to price your items appropriately and will also be able to decide on what can be sold and what needs to be discarded.

STEPS TO SELLING ON AMAZON

Choose Your Niche

Any new venture must start with careful and thorough research, which might be time-consuming. Trust me; it is worth every second you spend. Once you choose your niche, you will be able to come up with ideas easily.

Think about your hobbies and interests. If you are passionate about fashion, consider creating your own fashion line. If you like artwork, you can have your own line of décor items. You will enjoy your new venture more if it is something you are passionate about. However, make sure you formulate your ideas in a way that they generate good revenue for you. This is important because, at the end of the day, you need to see results in the form of profit margin and growth.

Source a Supplier

You now know what you want to sell. If the product is something from around your house, this step can be skipped as you yourself are a supplier. But if the product doesn't belong to that lonely corner of your house, you need to find a supplier to source you the product as private label. These are manufacturers who make the product and sell it at a wholesale price. Sellers can then brand the product with their own label. Start looking for manufacturers who can supply you with the products you are interested in selling online.

Set Up an Account

You are now almost ready to sell, but first you need a seller's account on Amazon.

If you're just a beginner, opt for an Individual account. That said, if you're going to sell more than 40 items in a month, you need to have a Professional account. This isn't a site rule, but it makes financial sense for the following reason: Amazon charges $1 per item for an Individual account and $40 per month for a Professional account. So, if you're going to sell more than 40 items in a month, you might as well get a Professional account.

Once you're clear on what type of account you need, create it using your chosen email address. You'll then need to provide further seller information, will have to verify your identity, and finally, will need to provide a charging method. After that, you'll be ready to start selling!

Launch Your Product

Okay, so now you have the product, the supplier and a seller's account. Your product is on its way to the Amazon warehouse. Now, you'll need to optimize how you sell your product, ensuring you use keywords that help you attract your customers. Amazon allows one to four keywords based on your product's category. Adding target-related keywords allows you to be more specific with your product listings. For instance, if you are selling school bags, you can include the target keyword "students."

Use enticing images, catchy headlines and a solid description. It's important to do whatever it takes to get your listing on the first page for searched keywords. Some fundamental ideas and basic rules of using SEO apply to product listings. Always bear in mind that the title of your product listing is the first thing that you can use to catch the attention of your audience. This can be done by using strong, catchy keywords to inform and attract the target audience. It should make sense and convey the right message.

AMAZON FBA FEE STRUCTURE

By now, you know that working with Amazon can be really advantageous. However, Amazon itself is a business, of course, and has to charge a price for the various services it offers. Here are things that you must keep in mind while working out the seller's cost of your merchandise. There might be some variation in fees due to:

- Price/weight/size of each product.
- Duration the product is stored.
- Type of product.
- Change in Amazon fee structure.
- Addition/removal of fee types by Amazon.

While estimating the profit margin on each product you sell on the platform, also take into account all the possible charges levied by Amazon for selling a product using their FBA service:

Seller Account Fees – These are the basic fees for selling your products on Amazon. You can choose from the two pricing plans—Individual and Pro Merchant. When you're just starting a business using FBA, you should choose the Individual plan (this means paying Amazon a fixed rate at the close of sale for each item). With an Individual account:

- You're allowed to sell up to 40 items per month.
- An inventory management facility is NOT available.
- You are allowed to sell products only within certain categories.

Once you get the hang of it, you can upgrade your account to a Pro Merchant account. This means paying a fixed price to Amazon for selling each product using their service, which is slightly higher than what you would pay for the Individual plan. With a Pro account:

- You can have unlimited product listings.
- You can sell more than 40 items per month.
- You're connected to the order management and e-commerce platforms.
- You have an option for inventory management.

Sale-related Fees – As part of this, you pay an amount to Amazon when you actually sell products on their website. The amount that you pay varies based on what you're selling and the product's price. These fees are divided into three types:

Referral Fees – Amazon applies a referral fee (commission) on the sale of books and all other media items. This is normally a small percentage of the selling price of your item on Amazon, for example, 15 percent of the selling price of an item. There are two attributes that define the referral fees—the product category and your selling price.

Minimum Referral Fees – There is a minimum referral fee that Amazon assigns to some of its product categories. This is normally around $1-$2, depending on the category to which your product belongs. If there is a minimum referral fee applicable to your listed item, you will have to pay the greater of the two fees—referral or minimum referral, not both. You can see which product categories have minimum referral fees on the website.

Variable Closing Fees – This is a fixed amount that is based on the type of item that is being sold on Amazon. The variable closing differs for different types of items. It's a flat fee of $1.80 that is added on top of the referral fee of the product that belongs to the defined types, including media items.

Pick and Pack Fees – These are the fees that Amazon charges for FBA listings and is normally calculated according to the time a person spends on finding your item in their warehouse and packaging it for shipping. This is the price associated only with FBA listed items, and both Individual and Pro Sellers have to pay this amount if they use FBA to stock, pick, pack and ship their items.

FBA fees are based on the size and weight of the items, as well as the time of the year. The FBA fee structure is quite streamlined, and Amazon considers picking, packing and shipping under one heading and inventory storage under another heading. It includes the fees for boxes and containers, and it even covers returns from buyers. This component of the fees also depends on the size of the product you're going to store and ship. FBA products are divided into two types based on the size of packaging:

Standard-sized products—these are standard-sized items that are fully packaged and weigh less than 20 pounds. The maximum size allowed for this category is 18'' x 14'' x 8''.

Oversized products—these are items with sizes that exceed 18'' x 14'' x 8'' and/or weigh more than 20 pounds.

Weight Handling Fees – This fee depends on the weight of the item being sold on Amazon FBA. If the item weighs more, the fees will be more, and vice versa. You might know how much your item weighs, but to calculate this fee component, Amazon will also weigh it.

Storage Fees – Amazon charges storage fees to sellers who use their FBA service at a rate for each cubic foot of storage space the item occupies in the fulfillment center. This fee varies with the time of the year the item is stored. For example—the fee increases during the months of October, November and December.

The Amazon storage fee is something every seller should be aware of because you might end up paying a huge amount which can eat up your profit margin; it can even cause you to lose money on your products. Therefore, it is recommended that you access the storage fees on a regular basis and adjust your strategy to maximize your profit margin. As Amazon grows, it needs to stay ahead of the game by keeping space open in the fulfillment centers in order to satisfy customers. As the business builds, the space fills, and space is in high demand.

There are therefore two types of fees related to storage that you should be familiar with:

Monthly Inventory Storage fees – Since space is at a premium in the fulfillment centers, the greater the inventory you store in the warehouse, the higher the fees will be. The storage fees depend on the daily average volume of storage space the inventory occupies in the fulfillment centers.

Long-term Storage Fees – On February 15 and August 15 every year, Amazon conducts a cleanup activity for its inventory to assess Long-Term Storage fees. Generally, Amazon charges a fixed amount per cubic foot of space occupied by an item that has been stored there for six to twelve months. For any products in the warehouse for longer than 12 months, the amount is slightly more. Long-term storage fees help Amazon to provide quality service to all their sellers and their customers.

WHY CHOOSE AMAZON TO SELL YOUR PRODUCT

More "Warehouse" Space

For large-scale sellers that want to work from home, the issue of warehouse space becomes an apparent thorn in their side. You simply cannot stock hundreds of items when your living space doesn't allow for it, and even if it does, it may make living there a bit uncomfortable. With FBA, this is no longer a huge concern since you will be able to ship all of your items to them in large packages, and they will store the items for you until sales are made. This means that your home isn't cluttered.

Access to International Marketplace

Amazon offers an international marketplace for you to ship to, and when you ship with Amazon FBA you get access to that marketplace without having to worry about varying shipping costs. Instead, Amazon takes care of that for you! Whether you want to ship to Canada, the United States, Mexico, or anywhere within North America. This increases your product reach and gives you even more opportunity to sell, with a higher number of potential buyers who may be interested in your products.

Amazon Oversees Customer Service and Returns

When you ship with Amazon FBA, Amazon takes over the responsibility for seeing to your customer service and returns associated with your products and shipments. This means that all you really have to do is pick products, manage production and manage your product listings. Everything else associated with the product and shipments is managed by Amazon.

A Prime Logo

All Amazon FBA merchants are provided with the exclusive Amazon Prime logo on their listings. This means that Amazon Prime members who are shopping for your products will know right away that they get access to all of their sweet membership-exclusive opportunities with your product listings. It is just like having a business-exclusive membership without having to oversee the membership program or processes!

Speedy Growth Opportunities

Since Amazon FBA oversees a great deal of the work involved with managing your products and shipping, it takes a lot of work off of you. That means that you can simply focus on choosing products and having them produced and sent to an Amazon FBA warehouse for Amazon to do the rest. Without you having to worry about so much of the business processes, you can focus more on the development of your business and getting the word out there! That means you can grow your business quickly and with minimal effort on your own behalf!

Easy, Cost Effective Business Model

When you are running a brick and mortar business, you have to worry about a significant amount of overhead. When you are running a regular online business, you still have a great deal of overhead when you factor in inventory storage and shipping costs. However, when you have an Amazon FBA business, your cost reduces significantly. Instead of paying for each individual shipment, and to store all of your products, you get to pay a single fee for all of this.

Inventory Storage and Shipping Services

As you have likely already gathered, the biggest benefit to Amazon FBA is that you have your storage covered and your shipping services covered. You do not have to worry about storing your products or ensuring that they are stored safely and appropriately. You do not have to worry about paying for larger storage lockers whenever your inventory levels grow or paying extra for storage space you are not using on months when you have less inventory. You also don't have to worry about paying the enormous tab that comes with running a shipment business.

Less Manual Labor

Perhaps more importantly, the task of selling products, packaging products, and shipping products is very, very time-consuming. This is especially true for those working alone. To combat this, the solution is a service like FBA. When an item is sold, they take your products, package them in Amazon packaging, and ship them to the customer for you. This saved time and workload means you can focus more on expanding the business and less on packing boxes and making trips to the post office or other carriers.

Fast and Free Shipping

One of the great perks of Fulfillment by Amazon is that items packaged and shipped by Amazon are going to qualify for their free shipping promotions. Currently, this promotion requires that customers purchase at least $49 of qualifying products. This often leads to additional sales. What that means for a seller is that those that handle their own shipping individually will often be passed up by the buyer attempting to purchase an add-on item to bump up the order total to allow for free shipping.

Sit Back and Relax

Another great perk of taking advantage of FBA is that you really don't need to be working at all to be earning money on the products you have already had shipped to the fulfillment center. In a traditional ecommerce setup where the seller is also the shipper, the seller cannot take long periods of time away from work since they cannot avoid the need to package and ship items. It doesn't matter if you're on vacation, sleep too late in the day to go to the post office, or if you prefer to spend your time at the bowling alley instead. As you're sitting around enjoying a cold beverage and a good meal, Amazon is selling and shipping your products on your behalf. For those that wish to setup multiple income streams or are still working a "real job," this means that you're effectively still earning so long as there are still products at the Amazon warehouse that are selling. Doesn't that sound nice?

Fast and Timely Delivery

Delivery time is one factor that will sometimes make or break a sale. Customers buy items online and they want these to reach them in the shortest amount of time. With Amazon FBA, your items will have the benefit of faster shipping times. This faster delivery time is attributed to your items being eligible for Amazon Prime; it gives your items a free two-day delivery feature. On top of that, it will also make your items eligible for 24/7 customer service and delivery tracking.

Simplicity

The interface that Amazon uses is favored for its simplicity and reputation. If you compare this to any other popular ecommerce website, you will notice that Amazon's platform is far superior, efficient, and well-suited for all professional sellers. You won't need to deal with different platforms like PayPal. You can easily eliminate the hassle of shipping the products yourself and managing your listings and your fees. You don't even have to shoot photographs of the products yourself. Amazon makes life simpler for a vendor.

Good Pricing

Amazon helps to get the best prices that you possibly can for your products. This is because of Amazon's Average Selling Price (ASP), which is higher for most items, even more so for all those products sold through FBA (Fulfillment by Amazon). A really good thing about the customer base on Amazon is that most of the customers are looking for ease of shopping and multiple options, and not just for products that are low priced.

Visibility

Every seller starts out as a small seller and will still be a part of the entire system. Amazon offers much better visibility to a small seller than any of the other platforms. Amazon makes use of rotating search results, which is a great way for new sellers to get some exposure. It also provides the option of buying sponsored links to increase traffic.

3. CREATE AN AMAZON SELLER ACCOUNT

T his is it! Start your selling business with signing up with Amazon.

Amazon.com is the marketplace in selling your products around the globe, and everything begins through creating a seller account with Amazon. Whether as an individual or professional, you have an easy access to Amazon that enables fast selling online.

Get started to sell on Amazon with no need of having your own website! Just do a self-registration process at **Amazon Services Seller Central** site, without talking to any salesperson.

Before I give you a step-by-step guide on how to create your Amazon seller account, here is a list that you'll need particularly for Professional Seller account:

- Business name, address, and contact information
- Credit card with valid billing address and is internationally chargeable
- Phone number (you'll be reached here during the registration)

- Tax identity information

AMAZON SELLER TYPES

As mentioned, when you sign-up with Amazon, you have to select which seller account type you prefer, either Professional or Individual. Each account type has corresponding plan and features.

Individual Seller

With an Individual plan, a seller is spared from monthly selling fees except for the commission that Amazon gets from each item sold. This option is usually for sellers who plan to sell less than 40 products a month.

If at the start, your budget is insufficient or you want to start slow and build your inventory cautiously, you may opt to register as an individual seller. You will only be charged for every successful order. You may always upgrade to Professional, if necessary.

Professional Seller

The Professional plan is based on a monthly fee. It is suitable for sellers who plan to sell an unlimited number of products. Sellers are also allowed to list products not currently being sold on Amazon. This option is usually chosen by sellers who own offline stores and can sell more than 40 products a month.

If you prefer to have more features, then go for the Professional account. Don't worry if you change your mind later. You can always switch from Professional to Individual account. Just change this from your account settings and all the features will be changed to an Individual account.

You have to consider that registering as a Professional seller, the monthly subscription is charged upon completion of registration, and so considering your finances is important. But, if there are current promotional offers, you may want to consider getting the offer.

I advise that at the start of your registration, get to know the **other fees** to be charged when an item sells. This is also very important to review when calculating how much you will sell a product.

HOW TO SET-UP AN AMAZON SELLER ACCOUNT

Here's a guide to sign-up your seller account on Amazon:

Step 1: Make sure you have decided which seller type you want to register when you open your browser to this site http://services.amazon.com/content/sell-on-amazon.htm. If you're not from the US and want to register locally, check the flag/country choices at the right upper corner of the page to ensure that you will be registering at the local Amazon site. It will redirect you to a local Amazon site.

Step 2: Select the seller account type by clicking the corresponding button, Professional or Individual. You may want to view the available and eligible categories, before clicking on the button to check the variety of product categories that you may list with each account type.

Step 3: Fill out relevant information. On this page, keep your eye on the

Amazon Services Agreement. Take your time in reading it before checking the box that you have accepted the terms and conditions.

Creating an account as an Individual seller has somewhat a straightforward process with less information needed unlike registering the Professional account.

Just a bit of suggestion when making your Store Name, think of a name about "quality deals" so that your Amazon Storefront would reflect a shopper friendly store. Add to your name word/s like Best ever, Deals, Discount, Quality, for less, Specialty, Fast, Great and the like that you can think of.

Step 4: When you click the "Continue" button, you'll provide the information needed for phone verification. Choose whether you want to be called or sent a text message to the phone number you entered. You'll be given a 4-digit pin which you will type in to verify your identity.

Step 5: Click the "Register' button and your registration will be complete.

4. IDENTIFY PRODUCTS POPLE WANT TO BUY

D eciding what you sell is extremely important as it will influence the type of marketing you will want to try further down the line and also determine where you can go to source the things you want to sell. In general, you want items that are specific enough to not already have thousands of online stores already filling the niche, while at the same time broad enough to still see traffic from general Google searches. The right mix can be tricky, but you'll know it when you find it.

CONSIDER THE DEMAND

One of the first things you will want to consider is whether you have the knowledge about your chosen niche that is currently being underserved by the online community. For example, if you really enjoy knitting and know that alpaca wool yarn is the best, then consider selling it if it is relatively hard to find currently. Everyone is part of a niche if you try hard enough, take the time to think about the items you buy regularly that are either hard to find or wear out extremely quickly, it can help to write the ideas down as you think of them, so you don't need to work through the entire process with each, ruining your brainstorming flow.

Private label basics

When it comes to creating your own private label there are a few things you are going to want to keep in mind to ensure you get into the private label FBA business with the proper mindset. This means that the first thing you need to consider is the amount of capital that it is going to require in order to create your initial product line. It requires a significant amount of capital to get your own private label up and running and the larger or more complicated your product is the greater those expenses are going to be. If you are interested in getting started selling on Amazon on the cheap, retail arbitrage is more your speed, to create a private label you have to be willing to spend.

Deciding if your product is a good fit for a private label

Once you've done some research and determined what niche is going to likely be a good fit for you, the next thing you are going to want to consider is if the market is favorable when it comes to private labels. The first thing this means is determining if there is one or more national brand in the niche space that already dominates the space. This means you will naturally be limited in what you can choose, though you can likely find a sub niche that is more agreeable to private labels if you try hard enough.

- **Design the right logo:** When it comes to designing a logo, it is important to consider what you ultimately go with long and hard as your logo is going to be seen more than any other aspect of your business. When it comes to finding the right logo for you, a good place to start is with common symbols as when done properly your logo will spring to mind whenever that symbol is used.

- **Choosing a name:** While it doesn't take much to pick out a bad company name when you see it, understand what it takes to create a good name can be much more complicated. To get started, you may want to consider which of the three primary name conventions, whimsical, evocative or descriptive, that you want to explore more fully.

- **Know what's popular:** When it comes to creating a useful business name, it will automatically make it easier for you to attract new customers if people can find your business by simply searching for whatever product or service it is that you provide.

- **Consider related words:** If you don't have anything catchy in mind right off the bat, the first thing you are going to want to consider is words that are naturally related to the product or service that you want to provide.

AMAZON PRODUCT RESTRICTIONS

It is also important to keep in mind the Amazon FBA Product Restrictions, so you won't waste your time scouting for products, and later on discover that Amazon won't approve your listing. Here's the list of product requirements and restrictions you should be aware of:

- **Categories for Approval -** Know the checklist that will guide you on how to list products into appropriate product categories.

- **Labeling of Date and Temperature Sensitive Products -** Know how to prepare products with expiration dates both for human and animal products (e.g. ingestible and consumable products)

- **Restricted Products** - You should be guided by the laws and regulations of the product you will sell. Any illegal and unsafe products are prohibited, and if you have listed such products, your Amazon account may be suspended or terminated without reimbursing any unfulfilled inventory.

- **Hazardous Materials and Dangerous Items** - Any product that belongs to this category (e.g., explosives, aerosols, poisons, vehicle tires)

5. FIND HIGH QUALITY PRODUCT SOURCES

F inding the right supplier or the right wholesalers for your Amazon FBA business is imperative, meaning that you can't "cheap out" or not care about this aspect. As you can imagine, your business will revolve around your supplier quite heavily. Truth be told, if you don't have any products that you can sell, then it would honestly be impossible for you to make any money which would, therefore, equal no profits. On the other hand, if you decide to "cheap out" and sell low-quality products, chances are people will return the products. Even though we discussed the importance of finding a proper niche and the importance of advertising the product the right way etc., this can't be overridden by an unreliable or a cheap, low-quality product.

FINDING SUPPLIERS FOR YOUR BUSINESS – DEALING WITH DISTRIBUTERS

Finding the right supplier for your Amazon FBA business purposes is imperative for both quality purposes and shipping purposes. Now, if you are going to be using Amazon FBA or a similar type of Amazon FBA method, then shipping times do matter in order for you to stock up your products, but it isn't the biggest of the deal for that Amazon FBA model when compared to Amazon FBA methods using Shopify. Now with all that said, quality is the biggest factor you have to worry about when selling your products. So today, we will go through the top websites from where you can find great suppliers for your business. We will also talk about how to build a great relationship with them, and finally, for everyone using the dropshipping method online, I will reveal a secret to get the fastest shipping anywhere in the world, so your customers stay happy and fewer refunds are being made.

Online Amazon FBA

So, finding a supplier for people using online Amazon FBA as their business model could be challenging. Since most of the time you will be going by assumptions, your job is to take out as much of the guesswork as we can and find the winning supplier. Now, there are a lot of websites online where you can find products for cheap. But from my experience, AliExpress has some of the best quality products and shipping times. If you have been doing some research online, you might have heard things like "AliExpress is dead" or things of that nature. But I am here to tell you that AliExpress still works amazingly and will help you make some serious profits online. There are some tips and techniques you need to know before you fully start using AliExpress as your sole supplier.

Now, if you don't know what Ali Express is, then let me clarify it for you. Think of AliExpress as the Amazon of China. There are a lot of people selling products online on this website, mostly from China. As we know, most of the products are manufactured in China, meaning the mark up on the products will be a lot less. You can easily sell these products online for a higher price in the North American market. To make things even better, the products on AliExpress are mostly similar types of products which are sold or are popular in the North American market. The point I am trying to make is this; people selling on Ali Express are selling especially to people who want to start their Amazon FBA business.

There are some guidelines you need to follow before you start to use AliExpress to dropship products from, as there are some flaws. The things we need to look into before we start selling products using Ali Express are:

- Suppliers reviews
- Product photos and description
- E-packet
- How many orders sold

Now, if all of these points are checked out and prove good, then your supplier is good. So, let's begin with the supplier review. To find out if the supplier is good, the first thing you will need to do is check the reviews. Make sure the review on his or her store is at least 95% positive. If that's not the case, then either the quality of the product isn't good, or the product is something else when it gets delivered. Another thing to worry about is photos and the description. If the product has great photos and descriptions, then most of the time it shows that the seller actually cares about what he or she is doing and will do whatever it takes to keep his customers happy.

Another thing to take care of is shipping. If the seller offers a shipping method known as e-packet, then the shipping times will be a lot faster than other suppliers. Normally, e-packet delivers the product in 2-3 weeks, which is the fastest shipping time you will get on Ali Express, so make sure your supplier provides you with e-packet. Also, to make sure this supplier is reliable, check out how many orders he/she has had. If it is higher than 500 orders, then they are in the clear. If all the points I just described to you checked out well, then the supplier is a good supplier and you can truly start to grow your business with him or her. And if the supplier doesn't check out on all these points, then find a new one.

One more tip I would share with you; Ali Express tends to take some time when processing a payment. It could take up to three days. It is done simply for their security. If you want to expedite the process of payment for your order to be shipped even faster, then I would recommend using Ali pocket. Ali pocket is similar to a gift card. It is like a safe credit card for Ali Express, so if you buy Ali pocket in bulk and use it to buy the product which you will be shipping out to your client, no time will be wasted processing payments and the order would be shipped right away.

Now, AliExpress is great for selling new trending stuff. But if your goal is to sell fan t-shirts and things of that nature, then it might not be the right choice for you.

AliExpress has a lot of things to sell online, but the products it sells are not specific to niches and people. This is where print-on-demand t-shirts come in.

What is print-on-demand, you might ask? Well, print-on-demand is a service where you come up with a logo. Pick out a plain t-shirt sweater or whatever they have, then the company will use your logo and put it on a t-shirt, etc. and directly ship it out to the customer or the buyer. That is what print-on-demand is. Now, there are a lot of websites to choose from. But the one I highly recommend is Pillow Profits. It is amazing - not only do they have your good old t-shirts, but they also offer things like pillowcases, shower curtains or bedsheets which can be sent to a customer with your logo on any of those things.

Now print-on-demand is ideal for those super niche fan pages we talked about before. Since those fan pages are unique and hard to find, you need to be really unique with your products just like the pages you are promoting it to. So, if your store is based on super-niche products, then it would be hard to find products on Ali Express and this is where print-on-demand comes in.

Most of the print-on-demand websites have a really fast delivery since most of them are based in areas out of the United States. So, you don't need to worry about shipping or any of that. Just make sure to pick out a print-on-demand website you like and come up with a logo.

Let's talk about building relationships with your suppliers. It is imperative that you build a great relationship with your supplier. Not only will it help you make more profits, but it will also help you get faster shipping times. What I am about to tell you applies more to AliExpress rather than print-on-demand websites. Regardless of which website it is, you need a great relationship with your supplier. So, in order to build great relationships with your suppliers, here are the ways you can do so.

- Give them business
- Be accepting
- Leave them great reviews

Giving them business is quite self-explanatory. If you want to build a great relationship, you have to give them business. You can't expect to be their "special customer" if you don't buy anything from them. So, make sure you first buy at least 20-25 items before you can think about asking them for a discount on your products. Another thing to be mindful about is making sure you don't get angry at them for a shipment which is a couple of days late or things of that nature. You have to remember that they are trying their best to keep you happy, just like you are trying to keep your customers happy. So, make sure you are being accepting and not making a big deal about small things like these. The final thing is to leave a positive review because let's face it, everyone cares about positive reviews. If you follow all these steps, you will start to build a great relationship with your supplier, and you can slowly start to ask for things like discounts on your orders which would mean higher profit margins for you. So, make sure you start to build a great relationship with them.

With all that said, that is all for finding a supplier for people using online Amazon FBA. Let's talk about finding suppliers for people using Amazon FBA or warehouse Amazon FBA. It is a little bit different but shares some of the same principles.

Warehouse Amazon FBA

To find suppliers or products for this type of Amazon FBA is a little bit easier when compared with online Amazon FBA. Since you can inspect all the products before you start selling, it makes it one step easier. So, in short, there are three ways you can go about finding a supplier. The first one is using sites like AliExpress. The second one is to find a warehouse where they are selling the products for cheap, and finally, buying products in special sales and reselling them.

Now, you already know how to find the right supplier on AliExpress, but let's talk about how you can use AliExpress for warehouse Amazon FBA. So, right off the bat, once you find a product that you would like to sell, I would highly recommend you buy one of the products and really check its quality. Once you have checked it out and made sure that the quality is of a high caliber, then you should contact the supplier and work out a deal. You see, since you will be buying the product in bulk, there will be higher chances of you getting it for a further discounted price, so make sure you ask for it so you can make even more profit. Finally, once that is all done, ship it to the warehouse and start selling.

That was using AliExpress. Now, let's talk about using warehouses or special sales to find your supplies. People don't realize that there are a lot of warehouses like Costco where you can buy stuff for cheap and sell it on Amazon. The way this process works is simple. Go to a warehouse such as Costco, find a product in bulk for really cheap, and then transport it to Amazon's warehouse and start selling. Trust me, I have found so many cheap products in Costco for sale which have made me some great profits! Make sure you find these products and start selling them on Amazon.

Finally, one of the ways I have made tremendous amounts of money on Amazon FBA is by waiting for sales like Black Friday and things of that nature. I would buy products on sale for 50% to even 70% off and after the sale is done, I would sell it on Amazon at its original price. Although this method is not as frequently occurring as the other two, it will yield you a lot of profits so make sure you wait for these sales to make some real cash.

Most of the time, you will find brand new stuff for sale near you, and the seller will be selling it off for next to nothing. So, this would be your time to shine. Find something in bulk for really cheap on these websites. Work out a deal and sell it off on Amazon for a great profit. Now if you found something for cheap but the quantity is low, then I would recommend using eBay to sell it on.

To conclude this chapter, I would just like to remind you how important it is to have the right supplier. A great supplier can either make your business or break it. Making sure you have the right supplier is imperative as it will help you have a longer sustained business.

Where to Source Products That You Can Resell Big Profits

Making profits and that too, big profits is the priority of any individual who would invest money and time online. You just need to remember one thing-buy low and sell high! For this purpose, you need to source your products for lowest prices possible. Retailing and wholesaling is not new to the world. It has been there for thousands of years. Only the currency has switched from animals to consumables to paper to e-money.

There is one more difference that has come between the ancient times and the modern times. The secret of retailing used to be closely guarded by a few people earlier before the advent of Internet. But now, it has become the part-time and full-time occupation of hundreds and thousands of Internet users. There is one more reason behind this sea change-the new economy. Things are easily available now than they ever used to be.

Where you can find your merchandise to sell on Amazon

This is not a secret anymore that Amazon is an ideal place to make money online because of the vast array of customers available round the world. But not everyone knows where to look for buying products before you plan to sell them. You do not need a magic wand to source cheap products. Just be aware and keep your eyes and ears open all the time. Do not miss a single opportunity if possible. You cannot just go to someone and ask for their sources. They are never going to part with their hard-earned sources. Let us take a look at some of the sources which you can utilize to make money on Amazon.

Contact manufacturers

You can find some manufacturers online and ask them to quote a price. There are many manufacturers who are willing to find traders online and sell their products in different markets. You may find a manufacturer or a firm which is producing some products in, say, China and are selling them at extremely cheap prices. If you observe that the demand for the same product is high in your country, you can make use of the opportunity. Also, keep in mind that you eliminate the middlemen from the chain of sale and contact the manufacturer directly. This will save you a lot of money on your purchase and hence, you will make more profits.

If you know a startup or any other local company which has not yet entered the online marketplace, you can also contact them and procure merchandize from them.

6. TOOLS THAT YOU WILL NEED TO GET STARTED

T o get into flow with this business with Amazon, you must have some essential things handy. These supplies and tools will make your business easier and you will also earn more with time. However, it is not necessary that you must procure these tools in the beginning of your business. Moreover, many of these tools are tax deductible. Thus, you can take the help of these tools for last minute tax deductions. That is good news! Isn't it?

INVENTORY LAB

Inventory lab is a web application which runs separately from your internet browser. Though it can work with any operating system and computer, it is recommended that you use it with at least Internet Explorer 8 and a modern browser. The application will support your work in terms of innovation and customer service. Inventory lab is capable of handling monthly profit/ loss, goods sold, etc.

HELIUM 10

If you want a product that is a comprehensive suite of tools for Amazon sellers, go for Helium 10. It's one of the most popular Amazon competitor research tools available on the market, and It's perfect for product development, keyword listing, and optimization. You can easily outrank your competitors and find profitable keywords and products.

SCOUTIFY

This application deals with scanning of items you list on Amazon. You will find Scoutify as a part of the previous application, Inventory Lab. The user interface of Scoutify is very simple to navigate. You will also find many features that will make your scanning portion of the business simpler than ever before. One exciting feature of the app is that if you receive multiple results after scanning an item, you do not have to scan the product again. You can simply go back to the results to verify the duplication of results.

JUNGLE SCOUT

Jungle Scout is a great Amazon product research tool if you need to monitor the competition, estimate revenues, and filter through millions of products until you find the best for you. Additionally, Jungle Scout has a useful Chrome extension to validate your product ideas basing on the data that matters most.

GUMMED TAPE DISPENSER

An efficient tape dispenser is indispensable when you are working with someone as big as Amazon. Your customers will be pleased when they see the product packed in a professional manner. The recommended product to buy is Better Pack 333. The product is a gummed tape dispenser. Recall the kind of tapes on the packages of Amazon. This tape dispenser gives you the same kind of tapes. You will need only one portion of tape on both opening of your box. The dial on the tape dispenser gives you the perfect tape each time you enter the size of the tape required.

EBATES

Ebates is a Cashback website and helps you a lot in online arbitrage. You can install it in your browser bar which will constantly remind you to activate cash back if you are working on a retail website. Ebates is more reliable in terms of giving you Cashbacks in time, which many other Cashback websites do not do.

SELF-SEALING POLY BAGS

If you are dealing in smaller items like health and beauty items and groceries, you will definitely need a lot of self-sealing poly bags. You must keep bags in 4 sizes handy-8_10, 9_12, 11_14 & 14_20. You can get 100 of each size of these bags from Amazon itself.

PRICE BLINK

If you want help with online sourcing, this tool is indispensable. You can add it in your browser bar, and it will let you know about a product that you are searching for, if it is available for lower prices on other websites. Thus, you can also search websites that are not very popular for options of buying. It also notifies you of the coupon codes for the websites which you are currently using. Price Blink comes absolutely free!

DYMO LABEL WRITER

Dymo label writer is a very efficient solution for professional labeling, mailing and filing needs. You will save a lot of time with this tool at your disposal. You just need to connect this label writer to your computer, and you can print labels directly from Outlook or Microsoft Word and many other famous programs. The thermal printing technology of the product eliminates the expense of toner or ink. You can also print expiration dates on grocery items and do many more things with it. Look for this product in a yard sale to save money.

LASER PRINTER

A printer is an equally indispensable tool like a scanner. And, if it is a laser printer, nothing like it! It prints your papers quickly and saves you a lot of money since you do not have to buy ink frequently. You can even buy a wireless printer if your pocket allows. There are a lot of things to be printed in a business and a printer makes your business simpler.

SCOTTY PEELERS

They come in handy, really handy if you deal with liquidation products, or cut down boxes, or open cartons of online sourcing; which is quite obvious that you will do in Amazon FBA. You can even buy multiple Scotty Peelers and you will never have enough of them. The metal peelers are better than the plastic ones.

AMAZON SELLER APP

You can use this app to find out the probability of profits when you are making a purchase. It gives you comprehensive information about the number of sellers for the item that you are planning to list, the sales rank or if Amazon itself is selling the product. Thus, it helps you take a better decision in all aspects.

7. LAUNCH PRODUCTS WITH AMAZON

With everything in place and your products arriving at Amazon's warehouse, it is time for you to launch your products! Launching products on Amazon is actually incredibly simple, but it does take some practice to memorize each of the steps and have a big impact on each launch. As well, you will find that each launch grows as you go because you are better at it each time, and you already have some credibility established around your brand and your reputation. The momentum between your own knowledge and this recognition will help each launch do better than the last, so long as you grow with the momentum.

As you launch your first products, follow this sequence exactly so that you are able to get everything done. Make a note of anything you feel you could do differently to accentuate your strengths and do better, though, so that you can create your own launch sequence that perfectly fits your business and keeps you growing.

OPTIMIZING YOUR LISTINGS

The first thing you need to do to launch your product on Amazon is to optimize your listing. Since Amazon works like a search engine, just like Google search does, using SEO is important. This will help your listings show up toward the top of the page, meaning you are more likely to get viewed over the people who fall later than you in the listing rankings.

The best way to SEO your product page is to use relevant search terms in your title and your product description, without going overboard or being spammy about it. Amazon actually has a clause built into their algorithm that prevents people from ranking well if they put too many keywords in their listing. Amazon assumes that these listings are spam and then ranks them incredibly low, preventing them from ever getting found by anyone who is using Amazon to shop. The key is to use keywords sparingly, and in a way that actually makes sense in the flow of your listing.

OUTLINING YOUR LAUNCH STRATEGY

Once your product listings are all set up and optimized, and your store is ready to go, you can outline your launch strategy. It is crucial that you do not start a launch plan until after your entire shop is set up and ready to go, as doing so could result in you not having everything ready come your chosen launch date. Pushing back launches to accommodate tech glitches or malfunctions is incredibly unprofessional and can massively destroy the momentum of your launch, so avoid that by preparing everything first.

With everything prepared, you can go ahead and create a schedule that will outline your strategy. Ideally, your schedule should include the date that you want your shop ready by, the date that you will start organic advertising, the dates that you will start paid advertising (and what types of paid advertising will be started when) and the dates that you will monitor your growth for important metrics in how you can improve momentum. Having all of this outlined in your schedule in advance will ensure that you know exactly what needs to be done on every day leading up to the official launch of your product so that you can stay on track and continue building momentum.

LAUNCHING YOUR ADVERTISEMENTS

Sponsored Product Ads

Sponsored product ads are the advertisements that are featured at the top of search listings when a customer searches for a product that they want. This type of ad is excellent to launch after you have officially launched your product on your store, as it will help your product appear over anyone else's in search rankings.

Sponsored Brand Ads

Sponsored brand ads appear the same way as sponsored product ads, and they work the same way, too. The only difference with a sponsored brand ad is that you are sponsoring your brand and not a specific product, so you are going to have only one single sponsored advertisement to reflect your entire brand.

Sponsored Display Ads

Sponsored display ads are the advertisements that appear on other people's websites, such as on blogs. Using sponsored display ads is a great way for you to reach other people's audiences so that you are more likely to drive traffic to your own page. You can create a sponsored display ad if you want to increase your reach with your Amazon store. However, the minimum budget for this option is generally $15,000, so it may be beyond most people's reach.

PROMOTING YOUR PRODUCTS

Promoting your products through paid advertisements is not the only way to get your name out there. Promoting your products on your own through word of mouth, known as organic advertising, is another powerful way for you to get your brand out there so that people can interact with your shop and purchase your products.

The best way to really promote your products and brand this way is to take pictures of your sample products and talk about them and demonstrate them for your audience. As you do, focus on building engagement by asking questions and encouraging people to follow your page so that they can stay up to date on your launch. This way, they are able to get early access to your products the minute they land.

REVIEWING YOUR PROCESS

After you have launched your products, it is always a good idea to stop and review your launch process. Look over how each step of the process went and jot down any notes you have about how you could have made it go better or what you can do it make it smoother in the future. The more you can keep track and adapt this process to fulfill your own needs and understandings, the easier it is going to be for you to have a smooth launch process that works every single time. This way, launching becomes easier and easier, and your products sell out faster and faster. As a result, you will be earning a far higher income in the end.

8. MANAGE YOUR SELLER ACCOUNT

MENU

The menu across the top of the seller dashboard holds links to most of the important parts of your seller account. Let's discuss each briefly to give you an idea of what you're working with.

INVENTORY

Under the inventory tab, which you should be familiar with already, you can view your inventory or add new items. The "Inventory Planning" link will take you to a page that helps you understand your storage costs and inventory available at Amazon fulfillment centers. It is a good idea to check this if an item has been listed for a long time. At some point, it may not be worth keeping the product stocked or you may want to drop the price to help move it so it's not racking up a large storage fee.

ORDERS

Since you're using Fulfillment by Amazon, the sections under this menu item are not that useful to you. Amazon will be handling the orders and returns of your items, so there's almost no need to ever use this section unless you decide to process/fulfill some orders on your own. There's no reason you can't do this and use FBA, but it usually doesn't make sense to do so unless it's a very heavy or large item that demands a lot of money and attention.

PAYMENTS

Under the "Reports" column, you'll see an option to view your "Payments." As your products sell and your account accumulates funds, this page will tell you when to expect payments and what to expect in terms of funds. Keep in mind that if you ship another shipment to Amazon for fulfillment, you will most likely be using these funds to cover the cost of shipping. You can use the dropdown menu to select the date range if you ever need access to old payments.

PERFORMANCE

This menu heading has a lot of pages under it, but all of them relate to your performance as a seller. For most FBA sellers, this is going to bode well since Amazon won't be shipping items late, usually ships items packed very well, and handles most of the day-to-day part of your business. Still, it may be worth taking the time to check out your feedback and see if there is anything you can do to improve how things are handled on your end. For example, if people are complaining that the condition didn't match the descriptions, you may need to revisit how you describe your items.

SETTING UP YOUR BANK ACCOUNT

Now that we've listed items and shipped them to Amazon for fulfillment, it's time to ensure that all of our financial information is in line. I highly suggest you do this sooner than later, otherwise any payments due to you may be delayed.

You will need to have two key pieces of data ready when setting up your account for payments to be made. These are your bank account number and your bank's routing number.

Your bank's routing number is always going to be a 9-digit code, and it can generally be found on a check, by searching the internet for "MyBank routing number" (replace "MyBank" with the name of your bank), or by asking at your local branch. Some banks use multiple routing numbers, so be sure to find the one intended for electronic transfers.

Once you have the routing number and your bank account number, go to your seller's dashboard and place your cursor over the "Settings" link to the far right of the page. From the dropdown menu that appears, you will select "Account Information."

You should see several links on this page, but toward the top will be a section for "Payment Information," and under this category you will see "Deposit Methods," which you will click. The rest should be self-explanatory now that you have your banking information.

INCOME TAXES

You may need to pay income taxes on your earnings. If you haven't input this information, you will likely be receiving a notification at the top of seller dashboard telling you that they need your tax information.

The link that's attached to this notification leads you to a page where you will fill out the information required for a 1099K. Current regulations on taxes only require that Amazon sends you a 1099K if you've made more than $20,000 in sales AND have had over 200 transactions. If you meet those qualifiers, Amazon sends tax forms around tax time, and you'll be required to input this income and pay your taxes on your profits. Having a good CPA may be beneficial and help you save money if you're selling in large quantities.

You can forego inputting your tax information if you're only selling your personal, used items. This is because it can be assumed that you're only selling at a loss. If it is your intention to quickly expand to selling new items at a profit, you should go ahead and enter this information. If you forego inputting your tax information now, Amazon will force you to do so once you've sold 50 items.

ALLOW INTERNATIONAL SHIPPING

Amazon defaults to sell and ship only in the USA for US sellers. However, you can setup your account to allow for international shipping. The best thing about the FBA Export program is that Amazon handles all those headachy customs and regulations that confuse many new shippers. Unfortunately, Amazon limits the number of categories that are approved for the Export program.

International sales can help you sell items quicker, and the downsides are minimal since Amazon charges the additional costs to the buyer.

You will be required to upload a copy of your signature, so if you don't have access to a scanner to make a digital copy of this, you may want to find someone that is willing to help you before you start to sign up for FBA Export. You should get a scanner, though.

EXPLORE YOUR DASHBOARD

While we've covered some of the major areas of interest, take the time to explore other portions of your seller dashboard as well. Amazon's setup is mostly intuitive and user-friendly, so it shouldn't take you long at all to become more than proficient with every tool at your disposal. As you build your business, the reporting and customer satisfaction data will be of the utmost importance for you to understand what is working and what isn't working for your FBA-based business.

9. AUTOMATE THE PROCES

I f you are introverted and have a dislike of face-to-face dealings with other people, then the next step is your product sourcing and supplier communications. Many people struggle in this area, and find it quite draining if you're new to business environments.

The challenge is that: your business needs to grow, and you've no choice but to continue sourcing new products, placing recurring orders, and negotiating with suppliers.

AUTOMATED SPECIALIZED SERVICES

When you have a team such as this at your disposal, it can allow you to step back from the negotiation process. Negotiation takes years to master, and this shows the size of discounts seller s can achieve. With high volumes of purchases, a service like this can (all but) pay for itself.

Teams like this can also do much more than negotiations and they can make a request for new product samples too. Additionally, they'll also work with your suppliers to deliver designs, based on your instructions.

A service of this nature can take a fair chunk out of your budget and should be considered carefully. It is more advantageous if you have larger (rather than smaller) shipments, so you would need to decide whether it's right for you Growing Your Sales

After you launch your Amazon FBA storefront, you are going to want to place your entire focus on how you can achieve growth with your store. Growth is how you can ensure that you earn a great profit and that your profit continues to develop over time so that you can earn even more with your store.

Growth is a simple process overall, but it can feel challenging, especially for new business owners who are still trying to learn the ropes of their business. As I mentioned previously, one of the biggest elements of success and growth is momentum, as momentum will give you the opportunity to keep developing over time. Momentum is the positive forward motion that helps you grow and keep going, and it should never be overlooked when it comes to generating success with your business.

In business, momentum is the key to avoid getting forgotten about or having people fall off before you get the chance to really build your sales. With momentum, people get excited and curious, and that excitement and curiosity continue to grow over time until you launch your new products or sales, and they have the opportunity to buy something new from you. This energy is important as it is what will keep you going, so make sure that everything you do is with the intention to build your momentum and grow the energy of your business.

In addition to building your momentum, here are some other tips you can use to help you grow your sales and earn even more from your Amazon FBA business.

FOCUS ON YOUR RANKINGS

First things first, you should always focus on your rankings when it comes to growing your Amazon FBA business. You want to focus on your product rankings and your seller ranking, as both of these are going to help you get in front of your audience in a bigger way.

Do What You Know

When it comes to selling on Amazon FBA, you are already likely wandering in a world that you do not yet know much about. For that reason, it is a good idea to do what you know by sticking with your strengths and selling products that you understand. Doing so can ensure that you are not adding more stress into the learning process, which will help make the learning process go even smoother.

ALWAYS TRACK YOUR NUMBERS

When people do not pay attention to their numbers, you can tell. Businesses fail when people are not watching the numbers because they do not have a clear idea of what is and what is not working. At the end of the day, all of the advice in the world will not give you a more accurate view of what you need to do to grow your business when compared to the actual numbers that you are receiving. Pay attention to them and use them accordingly, as this is your only way to track your momentum and guarantee your growth.

GROW YOUR ONLINE PRESENCE

A better way for you to grow your business and guarantee your growth is through establishing your own presence online and using your presence to help drive your traffic to your store. When you grow your own presence, you have greater control over getting your viewers to your store, rather than getting your viewers to Amazon central in general where you will then need to hope that they find your store.

Use Paid Advertising

Paid advertising is an incredibly valuable way to grow your online presence. Although it does cost more this way, it will support you with getting seen by an audience that you may not necessarily see otherwise. As well, it automatically improves your ranking results by putting you right at the top of the listings rather than you having to rely on organic SEO alone to rank higher.

ADD MORE PRODUCTS TO YOUR STORE

If you want to scale your business, one obvious way might be to add more products to your store. Having more products available for your customers to purchase means that you are more likely to have an increase in your sales because you are offering things that your audience actually wants to have more of.

10. CONVERT YOUR ITEMS

Whether you are on amazon or using any other platforms that contribute to the FBS, the original research that you do will help provide information as to if you should begin by buying certain items. When you set up your Amazon and multichannel pages you have two options. You could list a small amount of really good products, or you could list large inventory. You do not know which the best way is until you get out there and try.

You should look at the competition, which would include what they are selling and how many other resellers you determine are out there. You will also want to look at the model, year, size, availability, color, edition, price range, and condition, in addition to variables described earlier).

You may see that some products are in demand and yet that they are also available everywhere. In some cases, competition is good bur in others, an overkill of the same product is not desirable.

It is also a good idea to look at your competition and their shipping type and return policies are. These factors are beneficial and that just may give you an edge when you are ready to list and to sell as people love free and low-cost shipping

To do all of this initial legwork, you need simple tools: an obvious internet connection, smartphone or pad, some recommended Apps or other that you find, and/or a website to do some of the research mentioned prior. You can also talk to other retailers, and those who may be your sources for some advice on what the best sellers are or are not, and any product information or background that may help you.

INCREASING SALES WITH MARKETING

Pay-per-click or PPC strategies are misunderstood, underutilized, and if done well, will lead you to increase sales. Once you have your items have sourced, stocked, and listed you want to market them for sales. Pay-Per-Click advertising, better known as simply PPC, works by converting your advertising into sales.

You should always be looking for ways to grow your company. Here are a few suggestions for yourself.

- **Play on Your Strengths**: If you find yourself doing something you hate; you won't put your whole self in the attempt. Use your passion to create your business so that you are truly happy when it comes to putting in the work.

- **Graduate**: Once you get the hang of how the system works, gradually move to higher priced items. Set a goal for yourself that every year, you will venture into a higher priced item. Yes, they don't sell as often, but selling one item at a higher price may still beat selling 50 lower priced items.

- **Build Yourself a Website**- So now, you have your online store, but you still need more customers, and you are trying to build your brand. This is a great way to reach out to your customers. You can provide links right to your page, and you can create blogs, and posts so that you can interact with your customer.

- **Create Target Accounts**- Once you have your website up, you can provide a way for your customers to leave their emails. This way when you are having a promotion, a sale, or featuring a new product, you can email your customer directly with the link to your page.

- **Use Some of the Amazon Seller Tools**- Amazon offers some great tools for those who are building an online store.

WHY IT WORKS FOR ALMOST EVERYONE

Once you know how to source for a product, you are in the game. All other things will follow. You don't have to be a manufacturer or a producer. Majority of sellers on Amazon are not a producer; in fact, most of them are third-party sellers. Majority of those in eCommerce on Amazon are selling products that are related to electronics.

Here is another list of random facts about selling on Amazon that might interest you.

Products that are related to media and electronics are the hot cake; they take up about 50% of the total sales on Amazon.

- Furniture, other household items, and appliances follow at 18. 5%
- Food and stuff used for personal care come third at 14 %

- Toys, DIY, and hobbies take 12.5%
- Fashion is at 3.4%

With the above facts and statistics, you can see that there is an opportunity for what you are selling and if you fall into any of those categories you are very lucky.

Amazon FBA is one of many ways to make money online. The program was developed by Amazon to help sellers earn more and to build more entrepreneurs. Asides from FBA, here are the other ways people are making money on Amazon. Bring out your pen and jotter. Ideas are about to start flying in your head.

Private labeling

You will source for a product that has a huge market. You will make them available on Amazon, but you will label it as yours. Yes, people do that.

One thing about this option is that you are allowed to make an amendment to a product according to feedback and reviews your buyers make. For instance, if your buyers complain about the handle of a toy, you can use another design or type of plastic.

You can do this and still use the Amazon FBA. In fact, this is one of the best shots at making money on Amazon.

Retail arbitrage

Retail arbitrage does not need to change the labels on a product or make an adjustment on it and in that it looks like the opposite of the previous, the private labeling. You can make a lot of money and in millions if you are dedicated to this style of making money on Amazon.

Like in private labeling, you will find cheap products around you. In retail arbitrage, you will want to find the product in your location or somewhere not too far. The idea is to remove the cost of shipping goods to your location. For instance, if your product is in China, it will cost some money to ship it in. But if you are searching the Walmart store in your area, you will save yourself some shipping costs.

Literally, you will head to a local store like Walmart. Pick an item and compare its selling price to those on Amazon. If you see a lot of difference, with the ones on Amazon carrying the higher price, you have a business coming.

You will continue searching and finding cheaper products all around you. You will keep finding them, loading them up in your car and keep selling them on Amazon.

To make things easier, some sites have lists of the location where you can find liquidated sales at a cheap rate. Also, you can use some scanning apps to compare cost on both platforms before you leave the comfort of your home.

Earn as Amazon fulfillment associates

People who stay in a good location can capitalize on this option.

You will be assisting Amazon with packing, shipping, and sorting as the case may be. Your work is needed at fulfillment centers, delivery stations, sortation centers, Prime Now locations, customer service centers, and Campus Pickup Points.

You have a choice to either do this job as a part-time thing or as fulltime.

Amazon flex

This is like an elder brother to working as a delivery associate. Yes, you need to be in a very good location, and you might be lucky to earn as much as $18 and up to $25 for every hour of work.

If you have ever seen a guy coming with a package you ordered on Amazon, and he's not in uniform, that's Amazon flex. Your smartphone and a means of transport: a car, preferably are the essentials.

You will start by contacting Amazon that you want to take up this job as an Amazon flex. Once you have done that, you will follow the app religiously for instructions and guidance. You will acknowledge availability and flexibility for shifts. If you are lucky, you can finish your shift within a few hours before your period elapses and you will earn just the agreed amount.

Affiliate marketing

This is a viable means of earning a livelihood. You need to have a blog and a reasonable number of visitors who will click on the link to make a purchase on the website.

You are working as an advertiser. Your blog has a specific niche, say, soundproofing, and homecare. Amazon sells a lot of products relating to that niche. You will head over to the site and copy the special links and promote some of the products on your blog. Blend the links into your blog posts so that people click on it and make a purchase.

For every sale, you will earn a commission on every sale. The percentage is between 4% and 8.5%. You can earn a lot of money if you a large number of visitors.

The commission is not a lot of money. You need a lot of traffic and page views so that some of the many visitors will click and make a purchase. Without traffic or little traffic, you can't make much.

Amazon services

This option is for those who have a skill; you can fix things with your hands. This option is for you.

Let's say you are into cleaning, landscaping, etc. You will head over to Amazon and sign up for Amazon services. Amazon will connect you with people in your locality who need to have a clean faucet, a clean house, or some repair work to do. 15% - 20% of the payment will go into Amazon's pocket.

Publish books

Amazon is a large market for authors. Well, it started as a bookstore anyway, and now there is a large audience of authors and readers. Through Kindle Publishing platforms, readers can have access to a lot of books and make good use of their time. For authors, it is a medium to sell what they have worked for. Many people are making money from publishing non-fiction e-books, but fiction writers are the best earners on Amazon kindle. You know about a certain thing, and you want to give the knowledge in a book, say, art and painting, you can write something about it, filling it up with samples of your work.

How it works

If you are looking for ways to make money on Amazon, publish books in the categories and let people find it using keywords.

You will sign up for kindle publishing. For fiction authors, building an audience earlier is a good choice (blogging, Facebook page, Instagram). For non-fiction authors, you need to find a good idea and verify if there is a market for the idea.

For the writing part, you will need to do a lot of work, writing, and formatting your book. If you cannot write, do your research, make a bale of content, head over to Fiverr, Upwork or any other freelance writing website, and hire a writer to do the job for you. You will upload your book on Amazon using the appropriate format. And start selling.

Join Amazon handmade

It is for people who make handmade items like jewelry or bags. Amazon handmade lets you sell a lot on the platform with a huge market.

If you have seen other places like Etsy or eBay, you will understand this better. You are expected to make your product by hand – completely. How you go about it is up to you – how you arrange, craft, or assemble the piece is up to you.

You will apply for Amazon handmade and fill some simple questions about your product. In 30 minutes, you should complete the process and very soon order would come in for your handmade product. You will sell a lot with Amazon market size. You can also sell on Amazon if your product is already selling on Etsy.

Amazon Camper Force

This is targeted at RVers, people who travel and live mostly in an RV.

These people have sold their home and their properties and moved into an RV or a bus. They travel around, always on the move.

You can help those who don't have a permanent home address receive their orders when they order things from Amazon. This is necessary during holidays when there are more and more orders every day. The amount paid is dependent on some factors, and it is hard to get the full detail because it is not as common as all other methods. There is compensation for working overtime and bonuses for those who do the program for the whole holiday season. Amazon usually pays campsite fee if you work for the entire holiday (usually, from fall till December 23).

HOW TO BEAT THE COMPETITION

There is a lot of demand just as there is competition. If you know the millions of searches and sales Amazon receive every day; you will understand this is a vast and lucrative venture you can tap into. Amazon says it receives more than 90 million visitors in a month. Why? What are they looking for?

Obviously, they want to buy stuff on the platform. And that is your product and others' products depending on how you have presented them.

Another question you should ask yourself is 'why is there competition?' People can't be competing when there is no money to be made. Or you mean they are just competing who can display the most beautiful toys, bags, and appliances without making money. It doesn't work that way. For there to be competition, there is a lot of money to be made.

What you need to do to beat the competition is to find a product that will actually sell. If you put every other tip in place, then you are going to make money.

Amazon FBA is like retail arbitrage. You will find a cheaper product somewhere and sell it on Amazon. The unique difference is that Amazon is going to lessen the burden of work, including shipping and all that. It is real. It is worth it.

This capital is a little risk involved, like most venture on earth. For you to call it a business, there should be a level of an unpredictable future. Big investors also make big mistakes that cost them some of their money. This doesn't make them call the venture a scam or illegitimate depending on what it is.

Amazon FBA is legitimate; you can make money. The amount you make is dependent on you, the type of products you are selling and the demand for the product.

11. START YOUR BUSINESS

JUST STARTING OUT

Getting started with an Amazon Fulfillment by Amazon is easy, and it is much easier if you already have products that you want to sell or already have a selling account on Amazon. While you don't necessarily need either of these things to begin, you will eventually need them if you wish to make your Amazon promoting business truly work for you. The one thing that you do need is a plan for what you are going to sell and how you are going to sell it. Each of the following steps will give you the best chance at having a successful Happiness by Amazon account.

Business Structures for your FBA Business

When someone decides to start a business, one of the key decisions to make is what the structure of the business should be. Selecting the type of business structure can sometimes be really overwhelming, so it is good to know the pros and cons, tax structures, features, **etc.** that each of the structures can contribute.

The most common forms of business are:

- **Sole Proprietorships**: The easiest business structure to create is a sole proprietorship. The business is owned by one person who is the sole proprietor. In this type of business structure, there is no difference between the business and the owner in legal terms; it is meant for those who do business without any partners, associates or state and federal regulations. Some examples of sole proprietors could be freelance photographers, writers, graphic designers, etc.; essentially, those who work independently with few legal liabilities.

- **Partnerships**: This is a business structure where two or more individuals operate a business as co-owners. Each individual contributes property, capital, labor and expects to share in both profits and losses of the company. This type of business structure requires the individuals to file annual data regarding their gains, losses, income, **etc.** but there is no need to pay the income tax. All the profits and losses are passed to the partners.

- **Corporations:** Just like the LLC, corporations are created and managed by state law. But what differentiates corporations from other business structures is that it exists as a legal entity as per federal and state law. It is a legal tax structure and separate from the owners or individuals who control or run it.

- **S Corporations** – pass corporate credits, income and deductions through shareholders for the purposes of federal tax; they have a special tax status with the IRS. These corporations detail the flow-through of their losses as well as income on their personal tax returns. They are evaluated at their specific income tax rates, and this means prevention of double taxation on company income.

They are even liable to pay taxes at a certain level for passive income.

- **C Corporations** – are legal business structures that can choose to structure themselves to limit the financial and legal liabilities of their owners. They are an alternative to the S corporation structure where: profits are passed through to owners and taxed at the individual level. legal protection is provided due to limited liability but is taxed similarly to sole proprietors.

Research skills

You will need some time on your hands, especially if you want to sell a product that has a huge market. You will need to ask questions, notice what others are doing to make them sell more. In fact, doing research will give you ideas on what products to sell. You will find more information about this step when you read about creating a listing for products.

A brand

What made Amazon become so big and respectable? If you say 'hard work', you are on the way, say 'quality services,' and you are still on the way. But one thing is certain that makes them stand out from all. They are respected because they have put so much work in building up their brand.

Wherever and whenever you see their logo, just like Apple, you recognize them. It's distinct, unique. All those things you said earlier – hard work and quality services – are part of the things necessary for building a business, but you know it's more than that.

Get an Account

If you already have an Amazon promoting account, you are very well on your way to being able to do Satisfaction by Amazon. If you do not come with an bank account to sell your products on Amazon, you will need to make one. Start out utilizing the creating an account forms that Amazon created to show you what you are in a position to do. Make sure that you fill these out completely even including the bank information because that is how you are going to get the money when your customers pay out.

Find Your Product

Apart from items which are against the law and some which hold restrictions on them, you sell almost anything that you want on Amazon. This particular can be products that are handmade or were created by you. Individuals who use Amazon Happiness by Amazonoften have unique and handcrafted products that can only be found on their own Amazon . com page.

Ship to Amazon

After setting up your Happiness by Amazon account and accumulating all of your products, the next step is to get each of the products to the warehouse where they will be stored, selected and sent to your customers. This is an important step because, without it, your products will not be capable of being satisfied by Amazon.

Storing and Tracking

After your product has arrived in the warehouse, the staff will sort it according to your inventory. They might send it to another warehouse or centers depending on the demand in that location. As an example, if your product is children's toys, and Amazon observes that there is a huge demand for such toys in New York and Las Vegas, they will move some of your toys to the centers in those places, depending. This is one of the benefits of joining FBA as a means of improving your sales. This makes sales faster. This is happening with or without your knowledge or approval (now, you know, by reading this book) and it costs nothing more on your part.

Add to your listing

Your product is now in the hands of Amazon. It is now in their database that you have a product with them. You can start enhancing sales with promotions and advertisement so that you assist Amazon in its marketing strategy.

Essentially, you are helping your product by making people know about it. Don't ignore this advice on the certainty that Amazon advertising is enough. Although you might fold your hands and let Amazon do the marketing for you, it is not good advice. There are other sellers like you and if their marketing plans beat yours down, your products will left to wallow in the dark. As their number of purchase increases, people will notice their products more than others in the category.

Customer services

You and Amazon have a part to play here. Amazon is a reputable brand; they will follow-up on every shipment to ensure that customers are satisfied. If your customer needs an explanation on stuff, Amazon staff will be the one to handle it. Now, if they leave feedback on your product, this is where your attention is needed. You will need to make an adjustment so that good reviews will come next time.

Payment

Your payment comes every fortnight. All sales will be added up, amazon charges deducted, your profits will then be sent to your bank account.

As you can see, it is all easy and simple. Amazon is handling all the bulk of the work. This is serious business, and it should be taken as such; you should follow up and do your part excellently. Have you really grasped what you have to do?

An inventory strategy

Here is where you can make good money and lower the amount you spend on storing product with Amazon FBA. With an excellent inventory strategy, you will forecast the market demands and make an appropriate plan to meet it. It will also help you make a good guess of the quantity of the item to put in stock at a time so that orders will keep on moving promptly. Because if you put few goods in stock, your customer might be disappointed to find out the products are out of stock. They will move to another seller, and that might be the last time they will order from you.

Take Advice from the Right People

As you go into the process of growing your Amazon FBA business, knowing how to take advice from other people is going to be crucial. When it comes to mindset, being willing to take advice and find ways to grow your business through the support of others is also known as having a "growth mindset." This essentially means that you are willing to listen to other people and receive guidance from them that is going to help you achieve maximum growth in your own business.

List Your Products

Listing your products will be one of the most fun parts of the process. To list your products, you need to come up with a name for them, a description and tags for them which will help your customers find your products more readily when they are looking through Amazon.

Your products should have titles that are catchy, a couple days but tell the whole story of the product. The particular title should, obviously, match the product and may be able to be found if using the search engine. You can use the detail by detail process and template that is provided by Amazon to come up with the information and the tags of the item.

Market the Items

Naming the items and using the descriptions on Amazon is only half of the process. You need to make certain that you can market your products. Marketing can be done on both Amazon and other sites.

You can also market outside of Amazon. Let your friends and family know on social media that you have products on Amazon. Use your website to link to the products. If you are able to speak to people through any channel, let them know about the products you are selling through Happiness by Amazon.

Leverage Your Strengths in Business

In any business that you are a part of, whether its Amazon FBA or anything else, knowing how to identify and leverage your strengths is a crucial opportunity for you to grow faster. Every single person has strengths, and strengths of all shapes and sizes can contribute to the success of your business. Finding out what your strengths are and learning how you can leverage those to help you grow your business is a great opportunity for you to excel in your growth.

Build Your Network

Entrepreneurs value greatly from having a strong network, yet it is common for people who are in the entrepreneurial world to isolate themselves and attempt to do everything alone. For many entrepreneurs, they behave as if they have something to prove, and so, they struggle to really get ahead in their businesses because they are always trying to balance everything on their own shoulders. Although this may feel like the way you have to do things, trust that this is not the best solution and that growing your network and having support truly is the best way to go forward. This does not mean that you need to bring on any business partners or investors to succeed, but it does mean that you should have a strong network of people who can support you in cultivating success in your journey.

Always Keep Learning

As I mentioned with gaining advice from others, a growth mindset is crucial to your success. People with a growth mindset tend to be more open to receiving advice, are willing to find solutions to the problems they may be facing, and frequently look at life as a series of opportunities and lessons rather than a series of setbacks and failures. If you want to have the right mindset to succeed with your business, you need to always keep learning.

Know What You Are Planning

First things first, you have to know what you are planning. Knowing that you want to plan to develop an Amazon FBA business is a great first step in getting started. However, you need to be prepared to go even further than that. You need to know exactly what all of the steps are that go into planning an Amazon FBA business so that you are clear on exactly what actions need to be accommodated for in your plan, allowing you to achieve maximum success.

Choose to start your Amazon FBA business

- Identify how Amazon FBA works and educate yourself on the process
- Open your Amazon FBA seller account
- Brand your Amazon FBA store
- Discover what products you want to sell
- Source your products and have them approved by Amazon FBA
- Ship your products to Amazon FBA
- Market and sell your products to consumers
- Identify more products to sell and continue to source, ship, market, and sell more products so that you can scale your business

Create an End-Game Vision

Now that you know what exactly you are planning for, you need to create an end-game vision. Creating an end-game vision gives you the opportunity to have a clear focus for what you are working toward, which is crucial to your success. If you do not have a clear direction and goal for what you want to achieve, you are not going to stay committed because you will have no idea what you are working toward.

12. MARKETING STRATEGIES

There isn't a lot of marketing that you need to do when you are selling on Amazon since most of your marketing is done directly through Amazon. Still, you might want to consider doing some extra marketing to increase the likelihood that your product sells and improve your ability to make sales.

SOCIAL MEDIA MARKETING

This will help you get information out there quickly to help you make sales. At first, you will likely have a smaller following and it may be slower going. Soon, however, your following will grow, and you will have a healthy base of consistent followers to market to every time you are launching a new product or doing a promotion, or anything else that would encourage customers to buy from you.

If you are not savvy with the internet or prefer not to have to manage all of the work that goes into managing brand accounts on social media, you might consider outsourcing this. There are many people available for hire who can manage your accounts for you and post information regularly to help you get the word out there and keep your account active and your followers engaged.

INFLUENCERS

Whether you are starting a brand or not, having influencers use your products is a great way for you to make sales. You simply hire influencers from your desired demographic who have followers that match your target audience and send them a free unit of your product.

This allows them to test it and review it on their platform to their large following base, and often they can link your sales page directly to your account.

Influencers are an excellent opportunity to tap into a large following base that has already been established. As well, if you choose an influencer, they often already have the rapport and reputation built with their followers so that their followers know they can trust the influencer and their reviews. This saves you a lot of time, money and effort. Even though you are giving away product units, it can end up in you making a lot of sales.

PAID ADVERTISEMENT

You might consider using paid advertisement to encourage sales on your products as well. Paid advertisements allow you to create an ad (or have a professional create one for you) and then you can promote it within your advertising budget. The best opportunity is to promote this on social media so that you get access to several viewers at any given time.

WORD OF MOUTH

Finally, having positive reviews on your profile and account, as well as positive reviews around the web can really help increase your sales. This is why having influencers helps: they are trusted reviewers who can encourage people to buy through you.

In addition to word of mouth on the internet, you can always let people know about your products in person, too. Then, you can link them back to your Amazon account and give them the opportunity to buy through you. The more you talk about your product and you get others talking about your product, the more people are going to want to purchase it because they will want to know what all of the chit chat is about!

Marketing your products with Amazon is not as extensive as it would be if you didn't have amazon helping you. It may seem like a lot of work, but in reality, if you simply keep up with a few areas and do a few little things here and there, it can all pay off. Even if you are not interested in putting a lot of work into marketing yourself, you can always outsource the marketing to someone else who could oversee your social media accounts, or to influencers who will share your products to their existing following. You don't have to do a lot in order to get people seeing your product.

In fact, you don't even have to market at all. Though, it is recommended that you do so that you maximize your visibility and increase your sales volume. After all, if people don't know you have a product available, how are they going to purchase it?

13. WHEN TO AND NOT TO USE AMAZON FBA

T he best piece of advice is that you should try to verify the profitability of selling your product by employing a strategic process. You might try doing market research to know what people are actually buying. For instance, you can use an FBA calculator.

WHEN NOT TO USE AMAZON FBA

Moving on, here are other factors that indicate you shouldn't use the system. The risks are higher than the outcome.

You have a small number of items

You only have 40 pieces or less than that or the majority is on another platform, and they are selling fine. Then you should stick with that medium. Let others who have a higher number of items – in hundreds and thousands use FBA. The process of packaging items and moving it to Amazon warehouse coupled with Amazon charges and rules will not yield good returns with such a small number of items. The stress, return, and bureaucracy may not be worth it.

You have a small profit

It is good advice to do proper calculations if you want to sell on Amazon.

Imagine you are selling a product with a small profit margin. If Amazon deducts sellers' fees and the cost of keeping your inventory with them, are you still making a profit?

This could mean you are not making a profit at all. So, ensure you do your calculations. And you cannot increase your profit easily. There are competitions and price is one factor that can make a buyer scroll down to the next available seller. The topic about seller fees is one we will get to in this book.

Your product will attract more fees than average

Some products usually attract more fees than others, not because they are more valuable or expensive. These are things you should note about your products:

- Small
- Large
- Weighs a lot

Amazon will charge you more if your product is heavy or takes a lot of space. You should use the weight of your product to calculate the amount you will be charged as FBA fees then make a connection with your profit margin.

WHEN TO USE FBA

Your main sales platform is Amazon

If you have been using Amazon before, it will be good advice to join the FBA program. This will give you the opportunity to enjoy all the benefits of using Amazon's programs. For instance, you will be allowed into

Amazon Prime, and there is the advertising, among other benefits.

Amazon will handle other tedious activities. These include:

- They will help you source for new products
- They will help improve your listings
- It is their job to widen the customer base
- You have done your calculations

You can earn more and do less work when you have taken your time to calculate, and you have done adequate research. In this book, we will talk about the process of starting the Amazon FBA for success. With proper planning with the aid of the right information, you will be making a profit on the program.

Selling on other platforms which are affiliated with Amazon is a huge boost for sales. FBA will enhance the multiple channel or network and help you reach a wider shipping network. Amazon has facilitated the program with what is called Multi-Channel Fulfillment (MCF). This allows you to sell and ship on third-party platforms while using a third-party seller.

TIPS FOR SELLING FOR NEW AMAZON SELLERS

When you are new to something, you need guidance. You are in a new city, and there is no road sign, no poster to follow directions. Now a blind man is standing on the sidewalk with his little poodle. Would you ask him and expect directions to a place he has never seen before just that he has heard the sound of it?

That said, you need to be careful so as not to make mistakes. To that, here is some advice for beginners who want to make money selling on Amazon FBA.

Ignore the resources with outrageous ideas and success stories

You want to know what products people are buying on Amazon. You will find a lot of them, and many of them are already saturated. Many people will offer you the list of bestsellers on the platform for you to make your next billion. Follow it at your own risk. If you can't do something different from what the market is already offering, it is wise to move to something else.

Follow trends only if you catch the train early

There is a new trend on Amazon; you find it today; check the number of sellers you see on the platform; they are just five or ten or just a little. You are early to the party, so take a sit and ask the waiter for your own dish. Start selling the product.

Research like a drunk

Research everything and everything like a drunk. A drunk is a person who is not afraid to ask many questions, even the ones that seem stupid. But when you are reading and listening to the results of your research, you should put your ears down and dissect every piece of information like a toddler who has found a bewildering toy.

Sell only good stuff

So, you have a product, or you have outsourced a product, but you don't know if it is of good quality. You didn't use it yourself to determine if it is worth the money. Once you buyers find out you are selling a piece of worthless product, you are on your way to lose sales and with a lot of bad reviews. This could be the end of sales on Amazon. People rarely give a review on Amazon so ensure you are getting the good ones to avoid doom.

Source cheaper products

You need to do some calculations before you jump into the sales of a particular product. This will also help to ensure you will beat the competition with a lower price than others. On Amazon, price is an essential factor that can influence sales.

Sell products you are passionate about wisely

Although selling a product you are passionate about can bring a kind of joy, you should try to analyze the decisions you are making. When it comes to such products, sellers are likely to get emotional. They wonder why the sale is not moving in accordance with the level of passion they have. Well, buyers do not share the same passion, and you need to give them what they want to buy if you want to make sales. You need to be always logical about sales, not emotional.

Check if the product is patented

Selling a product that is patented is illegal. So if you are a private label seller, you must check if the product you are getting from a wholesaler is patented or not. This is something you must examine closely because the wholesaler will not tell you. Selling a patented product can qualify you for a lawsuit.

Do a lot of work on your product listings

Private label sellers are the ones that do their product listings. You are required to set up your listing and make it stand out. Start with finding a good product, you should always be on the lookout for the best products out there. Next, you will put that same effort in creating a listing that is irresistible for your buyers.

Stick to the rules

You will find out some sellers on Amazon are breaking some of the policies of the platform. They call it the 'black hat' techniques. They will increase sales by generating more reviews. They manipulate the process of reviewing a product. Some of them will get away with it, and you might be lucky or unlucky. Amazon will come down on you like a heavy rock if they find out you are playing games with their policies. They have intensified their strategies on finding out sellers who are engaging in review frauds.

You must improve your listing

If you are making sales, you might think your listing does not need readjustment. This is the first mistake most beginners make. Things can change over time; the keywords people use in their search might change over time. You have to monitor your listing and how it is driving results, especially if you are not making sales as expected.

Put your product in the right category

You might think your product has a better chance if you put it in a different category. Of course, you might earn the bestseller badge you are craving for, but you are missing out on some buyers. Why? Some buyers will go to a subcategory to search for a particular product, and if they can't find yours, they will go for the available option.

14. COMMON ERRORS

Not creating expandable brands and product lines from the start

If you are planning to build a sustainable business brand, you will want a larger umbrella of products to expand your business in the long run. Pick primary products that have plenty of complimentary purchases or can be bundled together with other items. This way you can keep adding items to create a longer product line under your brand. For example, if you zero in on the electronic gadgets niche, you may have a whole bunch of accessories and replaceable parts to sell to under a single business brand.

Underestimating the holidays

As long as you are comfortable holding on to these items for roughly 10 months, the deals you can find on decorations during the days immediately after most major holidays can practically guarantee acceptable profit margins on nearly everything you can imagine. What's more, by waiting 10 months before sending them to Amazon, you minimize your storage costs while at the same time taking advantage of all the people who like to plan for the holidays early. Alternately, you can wait until just a few weeks prior to the holiday to post your products and raise the prices even more to grab customers who waited until the last second and as a result, don't care about the costs.

Shady Reviews

Do not, in any situation, try to pay money to have fake Amazon reviews added to your private label products or any listing you've created on your own. This is usually easy to spot by Amazon, and even when they miss it, your customers often feel cheated once they purchase a product if it doesn't meet the expectations created by fake reviews. If you need more reviews, then you need to offer your product to people in exchange for reviews. Tell them that they can be upfront that they were given the product to review, and tell them that you're looking for honest reviews. If you are taking your time to ensure you provide high-quality products, you should be garnering good reviews anyway. If you have a number of bad reviews, take their criticism into consider and fix the problems.

Losing Money When Buying Overpriced Products

If you have somehow made the mistake of paying too much for a product, there are a number of options you have to attempt to make a small profit or at least avoid a loss. This includes:

If it is an item bought from a larger supplier or a retail operation, they may actually accept returns. You may have to pay a restocking fee or at the very least return shipping, but it is better than sitting on product you cannot make a profit on anyway.

Avoid the End of a Trend

One huge mistake people make is that they are far too late to the game on a trend. Catching a trend before it blows up can be a quick way to make a huge chunk of money, but if you're coming in at the tail-end of a trend and the market has already by oversaturated with copycat sellers, then you may find yourself sitting on product that's far too available in the market to really turn a profit. The time to join in on trending items is at the first whiff of their popularity, not after the market becomes so flooded that prices are quickly dropping. This is especially true of products that practically any manufacturer can make, as there will quickly become a ton of cheap options available.

Not Taking Risks Is the Worst Mistake You Can Make

You want to make calculated risks. Taking risks is what leads to huge payouts. A surefire product will probably sell well, but your profit is going to be very expected as well. You have to be willing to take a chance sometimes.

Not considering the demand up front

While selling niche items is a good choice, that doesn't mean every item is automatically going to be a winner. Once you have an idea of the general types of items you want to sell the next step is to assess the relative demand for each of the potential items in question. As long as the items you are thinking about selling aren't extremely obscure, this process should be relatively straightforward.

Not listing products, the right way

Even though we are told time and time again not to judge a book by its cover, shopping on Amazon, and anywhere online in general, is quite the opposite. One of the vital aspects of any listing on Amazon is the title, which informs potential buyers what the product is all about.

Not taking full advantage of images

Another important aspect of the product details of items on Amazon is the images included in the listing. They can cause shoppers to click on your listing just because of the quality of the image. That's why you should spend a good amount of time to research images that are top-notch.

Not using enough bullet points

If potential buyers fail to be swooned by your choice of title and images, bullet points are the next best thing to get a straightforward reaction. You have five spaces to include bullet points, but this doesn't mean you only have to use five words or even sentences. I personally use short paragraphs in each of those bullet points to home in on benefits and features of the item. Address common questions and objections as well. Use the first three points to showcase your products most pertinent features and use the other bullet points to answer common inquiries or customer objections.

Not pricing products properly

Opt to sell private label products that are priced above $10. Amazon lists items priced below $10 as "Add On Items, which means buyers cannot purchase your item by itself. They have to make additional purchases to be able to buy your product. Additionally, profit margins for products priced below $10 after deducting Amazon's fee can be rather low for building a lucrative, long-term business. You will need a very higher sales volume to witness recent returns. Ideally, pick products that sell in the range of $10-$30 for higher profit margins.

Not doing enough research

Another tip that many Amazon FBA users miss is that they don't do research on the Amazon site itself before deciding which products they're going to sell. Even if you enjoy fishing, this does not necessarily mean that selling fishing poles on Amazon is a decision that is going to lead to profits. Look at what's selling the most frequently on Amazon and take note of any markets that may look like they're being underrepresented.

Having too many similar products

Unlike the notion of a niche website that we've already discussed, you do not have to worry about keeping a product line that is similar when you're using Amazon FBA. Because your seller profile is not going to define the type of business that you're running, you have the freedom to pick and choose the products that you want to sell. This can be great for someone who is good at doing research on products within Amazon's website. By figuring out the profit margin that's possible from certain products that are on the market, you should be able to make better financial decisions for yourself and your business.

Limited knowledge of how amazon FBA works

Selling your products on Amazon is unlike any other place you can sell your products. Amazon can go directly to the Brand to source their products. You, as the Third-Party Seller are there to complement what Amazon has already put into place. You are an Ambassador to Amazon and are required to uphold every policy to keep your account metrics healthy, and active. Be sure to read all of the agreement policies before you create your account.

TO-DO LIST

Amazon Has Tremendous Data-Collecting Abilities

Amazon has tremendous data-collecting abilities. They can check every

SKU to see its level of popularity and see how well it is selling. They can check every customer's preferences. Amazon readily uses this information to plan for its own future sales. Yes, you are also in competition with Amazon, as an Amazon FBA Seller.

This information is not shared, and Amazon has the ability to take over top-selling products, previously only sold by Third-Party Sellers.

Since the products are all listed together, buyers can compare shop to see how like items stack up with delivery, pricing, and availability.

Amazon's Buy Box Algorithm

Amazon uses its Buy Box Algorithm to choose the seller that will sell their product when a customer clicks the, "Add to Cart," button. This Algorithm is so powerful that many sellers find themselves with tons of inventory because other sellers control the Buy Box for their products.

Amazon uses the A9 Algorithm to determine the popularity of the products sold. This is an organic algorithm that uses certain data to match customer's search results to the products they actually buy. More than half the battle you face selling on Amazon is making sure that your product is found. The more you know about Amazon's Algorithm, and the tools that are available to you so that you can wade through it, the better. If you are serious about running a successful business through Amazon, you will want to do everything you can to get this algorithm to work for you.

Here are some interesting facts about Amazon's A9 Algorithm:

- 70% of customers never click past the first search page.

- 35% of customers never click past the first product they find on a search page.
- The first three listings shown in the search results make up for 64% of clicks.
- 81% of clicks are for brands that were shown on the first search page results.

This Algorithm is used to show that their customers have a higher purchase intent. They are using Amazon's Search Engine to find products to buy. Amazon SEO is used directly to convert sales.

Amazon's Algorithm uses what customers purchase after they search to determine relevancy. It places weight on purchase behaviors such as conversions and sales.

Amazon places a huge importance on whether or not your customers can find your products. Customers use the search engine with keywords and phrases, that are then matched up to your descriptions of your product. They factor price, shipping, availability, selection, and sales history to determine how well people will find your product. This is why your SEO skills need to be in place so that you can be seen.

Tax and Duty Laws

Make sure you understand your State Tax Laws. You will need to make sure your State Tax is collected on the items you sell. You also need to remember to pay your State Tax as well. Talking to a Tax Professional may be in your best interest.

If you are selling products on Amazon that are imported from other countries, make sure you fully understand Custom Duty Laws. You will be fined by US Customs if they learn that you've imported items and did not pay Import Duties.

Learning Correct Behaviors for Healthy Metrics

Many people believe that there is a pie in the sky, and easy money around the corner. There is a way to be successful in business, and it can be quite lucrative, but you will have to put in the work to make sure that gets done.

Here is a list of the Correct Behaviors Needed to Be Successful with Amazon FBA:

- You must review, comprehend, and agree to adhere to all of Amazon's Policies.
- Do extensive research on the products you want to sell before you source and list them.
- Do whatever you can to streamline to process. We will talk about all the tools available in.

15. THE AFTERMATH

Your product is launched, and you are doing whatever it takes to promote it—running various campaigns, promoting it on social handles, **etc.** You are getting sales and reviews too. Now it's time to look at the aftermath, which is as important as other steps in this entire selling process. So, let us look at some of the things you should be doing post-purchase.

AMAZON PRODUCT REVIEWS – POSITIVE OR NEGATIVE

Amazon is a customer-centered platform. Your reviews on this platform transform sales into successes or disappointments at being kicked all the way back to the 20th page of product listings. When someone launches a product on Amazon, it is these reviews that tend to shorten the time lag between being "just another seller" to a "top-rated seller." Product reviews impact the conversion rate so much that they are a seller's powerful weapon to transform from "nobody" to "the world knows me." They impact the buying decisions of the shoppers and also act as good reference points for product improvement. Even marketers review them to understand the behavior and preferences of customers in the marketplace.

A seller should take several steps to stay competitive. He or she must provide

- A high-quality product
- fit-for-royalty customer service and
- an outstanding product page.

If you know these areas well, no one can stop you from becoming a popular seller on Amazon, assuming that you understand the basics around these three elements.

A weak point for every seller is negative reviews that buyers sometimes leave on their product page. Amazon never removes any negative feedback because it believes that reviews are meant to help buyers in making their purchase decisions and therefore shouldn't be tampered with. Being an Amazon seller, you must be mindful of any comments that your customer leaves for you, whether good or bad.

Although it is a tedious task, Amazon approves product review removals in two cases: Seller Feedback rating and Product reviews.

In the case of Customer Feedback, which includes concerns related to packaging, delivery, the condition of the product or product container and quality of customer service, FBA sellers can get negative feedback about damaged items or delayed delivery and these ratings hugely impact the overall profile of the seller and his business. In this case, you can absolutely get the negative rating removed as it is Amazon who is responsible for handling delivery, packing, shipping, **etc.** on your behalf.

If you receive a product review from a seller that has nothing to do with the product, it is definitely a removal candidate. Also, if Amazon finds the review to contain inappropriate content, promotional messages, offensive speech, hate content, promotion of unacceptable conduct or one-word reviews, it considers removing them from the product page. If an unhappy buyer posts multiple negative reviews for the same product (through multiple accounts), Amazon removes them.

Amazon encourages everyone to express their honest opinion for the benefit of other customers and sellers. Even if the opinion is in the form of a negative review, it is about his or her experience with the product, and these review comments are legit and acceptable on the platform. But if someone has formed a wrong opinion and is just trying to defame the seller, Amazon will look into the matter.

As a seller, if you feel you do not agree with the comment left by your buyer for any of the above-mentioned reasons, get in touch with Amazon. There are two ways to raise your concerns—you can report abuse and/or contact Amazon Seller support.

To know what type of reviews you are receiving, you must check them daily. After all, these customer reviews can have a huge impact on the success or failure of your business.

REACH OUT TO YOUR CUSTOMERS FROM TIME TO TIME

Post-product launch strategies should include taking required actions to proactively communicate with your customers via post-sale emails from your Amazon dashboard. This builds a strong relationship with your customers and lets them know you care about their experience. A carefully drafted, thoughtful, purposeful email helps you build brand awareness, boost ratings, increase the response rate and converts potential customers into repeat buyers. A thoughtful strategy should include sending out three types of emails to each buyer post-purchase:

Thank You

This type of email builds brand awareness, which is otherwise a tedious task, particularly for third-party users. By writing a thank you note to your customers, they will know they have bought something from a unique brand, setting a foundation for future purchases and converting potential customers into repeat buyers. Thank you, emails can do wonders for you and your brand.

Product Review Request

Amazon doesn't prompt buyers to leave a review for your product, so this is something you need to handle on your end. Encourage your buyers via a product review request email, asking them to share their experience of your product. This is an effective means of advertising for all potential customers who reach your product page.

Seller Feedback Request

Do not confuse Product Review with Seller Feedback as these are two different things. Seller feedback is the feedback your customer leaves for you, the seller. This feedback impacts the overall health of your account rating. These comments and ratings left by your customers can be treated as persuasive advertisements that can help build confidence in other potential customers, particularly those who are not familiar with you or your brand.

Check your Conversion Rate

Not just for Amazon, but for any type of business, the conversion rate is known to be one of the most investigated metrics to understand how a business is doing. First, understand that the conversion rate cannot be found under the title Conversion Rate in your seller account. Browse through the main menu and click on Reports. From the drop-down list, select Business Reports. Under the section Sales and Traffic, you will be able to see your daily business metrics which include the Order Item Session Percentage. This is the conversion rate. If you want to look at more meaningful data, look for the same column in the By ASIN report to get data for each item.

To understand how the conversion rate is derived, it is evaluated by dividing the Total Order Item (which is the total sales) by Sessions, which is the number of times customers visited your website/listing. This percentage is what gives you the conversion rate.

You know where to look for the conversion rate, and you also know how this conversion rate is calculated. Now it is important that you check and evaluate the rate on a regular basis as it helps you understand the success of your business.

Monitor Your Product across Social Channels

You have launched your product, so now focus on the people and not on the product. The emphasis should be on how the launch affects you and your business and ensure you know what people are saying about it on different channels. You can even use various tools, such as Google Alerts to monitor this kind of information. Once you see the response from your customers, take time to return a comment, not just thanks or sorry, but going beyond that to provide a full customer experience. If possible, subscribe to comments so that you can keep a check on any future comments they might add. This way, it will be easy for you to go back to those comments and respond. This will go a long way toward helping people understand how important they are to you and will build trust and increase profits and sales.

Monitor Your Inventory from Time to Time

Inventory management is important at each stage of your product selling business. It is essential throughout the year as the momentum might increase as you run various campaigns and marketing strategies. With time, you will see an increase in click rates, conversions and sales. If you do not have enough inventory to match the needs of your customers, the momentum is eventually lost, and this leads to a reduction in click rates, conversion rates and all that you have invested in advertising your brand. To sustain your place in the marketplace, it is important that you continuously monitor your inventory levels and see to it that there is no gap in your ability to meet the demands of your customers. Monitoring the inventory is particularly important right after you run a campaign and also during the holiday season as this is when more sales happen. If you fail to meet the expectations of your customers due to mismanaged inventory, you could lose out on some of the biggest opportunities of the year.

Here are some ways you can improve the inventory management process and organize your inventory effectively:

Use inventory management software

As an FBA seller, you can use any tools that are available to manage inventories that integrate with Amazon. These tools not only help you track your inventory but also provide real-time analytics about sales and conversion, which are important to give your brand a competitive edge. This way you will be able to better analyze the demand for your product and provide better service to your customers through tracking information.

Monitor supplies regularly

If your suppliers are not delivering your product on time, it can greatly impact your ability to manage the inventory. Therefore, there is a need to monitor your inventory closely on a regular basis to avoid delays in deliveries. Some of the key pointers you should watch for are:

- receipt dates
- agreed delivery dates
- quantity ordered
- quantity received and
- condition of the delivered package.

However, monitoring all this isn't an issue if you are an FBA seller as FBA automates the entire fulfillment process.

BOOKKEEPING

Most sellers on Amazon love to talk about optimized listings, product niches, etc., but when you turn the conversation to taxes, balance sheets and asset management, they shudder. This is because most sellers spend their time and focus on generating more sales, driving traffic to their listings, finding experienced private labelers, setting up optimized listings on Amazon, getting reviews and running campaigns, identifying demands, **etc.** But when it comes to assessing and managing the financial part of their business, they feel uncomfortable.

So, let's look at the basics of accounting and bookkeeping practices so that you can tackle the financial part of your business wisely.

There are two key financial reports that every seller on Amazon must be familiar with: the Profit and Loss Statement and the Balance Sheet. These tools will help you get to the heart of your business, which is financial statistics, and retrieve data that is essential to make key business decisions. Without these reports, you will not have a complete picture of how your business is doing.

Profit and Loss Statement

The Profit and Loss Statement is a tool to evaluate performance, and in large businesses, it is the primary and most important document used to show the capabilities of the organization. It gives the overall picture of what the net income, which is evaluated by adding all the expenses—your monthly Amazon Inventory Storage fees, expenditure on various campaigns and other marketing activities, shipping, **etc.** and then subtracting this amount from the total revenue. It is this net income that is needed to determine how much your taxable income is for the year.

If you are a seller on Amazon, this Profit and Loss Statement will come in handy when you want to evaluate your past performance. How did you perform last year? How was it compared to the previous year? While setting up this statement, you must remember to consider the type of accounting method you are planning to use; it can be either

Cash Basis

the revenue is reported in the Profit and Loss Statement for the period the customer pays the cash.

Accrual Basis – the revenue is reported in the statement when the business is owed money before the customer pays the cash.

The Balance Sheet

The Balance Sheet is used to evaluate the overall health of your business. The two statements go hand-in-hand. Only when you have the details of both statements, will you be able to analyze how your business is actually performing. The Profit and Loss Statement doesn't show all the components of the business; it doesn't take into consideration the amount you borrowed for your next order, the value of unsold inventory, sales tax you owe, **etc.** All this is covered in the Balance Sheet, which makes it unique as it is the only document that displays an accurate snapshot of the financial health of your business.

The Accounting Equation is a method that helps you understand the financial shape of your company and the way different components of a Balance Sheet are linked to each other. Based on the business structure, the equation varies from company to company. For instance, if you are the sole owner of your company and the Amazon seller, the structure of your business will be considered a sole proprietorship. In this case, the Accounting Equation would be:

Assets = Owner's Equity + Liabilities

Where:

Assets refer to your resources.

Liabilities are what you owe to other individuals.

Owner's equity is the difference between the two—assets minus liabilities.

A Balance Sheet is a two-sided document that lists assets on one side and liabilities and owner's equity on the other. As the name suggests, the aim is to balance both sides of this sheet, which means the total of both sides should be the same, confirming that the Balance Sheet of your organization is balanced.

Although the Profit and Loss Statement and Balance Sheet are two key documents for any business, there are a few other statements that are also taken into consideration:

Cash Flow Statement

A cash flow statement helps sellers understand the flow of capital that goes into and out of a business for a specific accounting period. This statement is unique because no other report captures the cash flow for a specific time frame. FBA sellers generally use this report quarterly.

Taking the starting cash balance, which is the company's total cash balance obtained from the Balance Sheet, all that flows into the system is treated as positive events and the outflows are negative. For the cash flow, the inflows and outflows are considered for three activities:

- **Operations** – These are the primary sources as well as the consumers of your business' cash. They include your sales income, income tax payment and the cost you pay to suppliers and freight forwarders.

- **Investment activities** – These are the selling and buying of assets which are not linked to the inventory.

- **Finance activities** – These include activities, such as borrowing money, taking a loan to pay for the inventory, repaying the amount borrowed, **etc.**

Now you should understand the important financial statements that you should be using to understand the financial health of your business as an Amazon seller.

TAXES FOR AMAZON SELLERS

Sales Tax

Taxes have always been a gray area for beginners as most don't seem to have a clear picture of how they work. Let us describe a clear step-by-step process of sales tax collection through your Seller Account on Amazon. Once you understand the basics, you will be able to determine how to apply for sales tax, how to set up your account to automatically collect the tax and how to automate the process.

Certainly, Amazon has given all of us a new way of looking at things— our shopping experience, buying things online, **etc.** It has also changed the way we used to think about taxes; Amazon has taken various steps to shield its FBA users from the long arm of revenue officers. With its increasing curve and need to have more investments in the organization, it has opened various warehouses. Opening these warehouses has required Amazon to state criteria for the responsibility and legal terms required to collect, file and remit sales tax. This criterion is known as nexus. It is the presence of a business within a state and something you would consider while looking at requirements to manage sales tax.

Income Tax

The IRS needs to know your annual income from your Amazon business, which means not just the cost of products but everything. You must take into considerations deductions like Amazon fees, Amazon shipping charges, FBA subscription fees, FBA inventory charges, health insurance plans, **etc.**

16. SECRETS AND TIPS

E very single new venture you take in life is going to come with lessons that you can only gain through hands-on experience. However, I want to help you gain this experience and grow faster by having an awareness of what lessons you are likely going to learn about and face in your Amazon FBA business.

In this chapter, I have provided you with the most important secrets and tips that you need to succeed that typically will only be discovered by those who are experiencing their businesses hands-on. Use these to help you get a jump-start and launch your business ahead of where most people launch, as this will give you the best opportunity to really help your business blow up right away.

ALWAYS FOCUS ON YOUR COMPETITIVE EDGE

Your competitive edge is your opportunity to really create the opportunity to set yourself apart from other Amazon FBA merchants so that customers are more likely to choose you over anyone else. Understand that no matter where or how you are promoting yourself, whether it is exclusively through Amazon or through Amazon as well as social media, other people are trying to access your clients, too. This means that you need to really know where your competitive edge lies and promote that competitive edge while also nurturing it so that you continue to remain competitive.

Learning how to nurture and promote your competitive edge requires some practice, especially if you have never run a business in the first place. To help you get started, let's explore what your competitive edge is, how you can promote it, and how you can nurture this edge so that no one comes in and sharpens your edge better than you do.

CREATE A STRONG CUSTOMER EXPERIENCE

When it comes to running any form of business, having a strong customer experience is important. When it comes to retail, your customer experience is not going to be as involved as the experience of someone purchasing a service. However, there are still plenty of opportunities for you to create a custom and enjoyable customer experience.

Creating a strong customer experience can be done by really considering what the process is going to be like for your customer from the moment they learn about the brand to the moment that your product reaches their hands and they begin using it. Being mindful about this entire experience will give you the opportunity to create an experience that is going to be enjoyable and memorable. As well, because you took the opportunity to create an experience that stands out in the first place, you will set yourself apart from other Amazon merchants, helping you stand out against the crowd and improving your competitive edge even more.

With Amazon, the best way to create a great customer experience is to consider what your branding and promotions look like. Believe it or not, these are a largely relevant part of your customer experience and doing them right is the best opportunity that you have to set yourself apart from others. You can customize your experience by creating graphics and descriptions of your products that are branded and that are enjoyable to read and engage with. This way, when people see your products and begin to read about them, they begin to generate excitement, and it becomes an experience for them.

LEVERAGE YOUR DESCRIPTIONS

Your descriptions are a wonderful opportunity for you to really boost your sales. On Amazon, many people open stores and upload generic, pre-written descriptions that are fairly boring. These descriptions are often direct and clear. However, they lack any personality and fail to really represent your brand or create something memorable for your customer.

To leverage your descriptions, all you have to do is customize your descriptions so that they are both accurate **and** enjoyable to read. Show your brand's personality in the descriptions by using words that are relevant to your brand and speaking in a way that is relevant to your audience. Using the same slang and words that they would use is a great opportunity for you to connect with your audience in a way that they understand and relate to, which helps you stand out even further.

LEARN TO TAKE BETTER PICTURES

When it comes to your Amazon listings, having the right pictures is crucial. Many people on Amazon upload generic pictures of their photographs that are taken from the suppliers and use these as their listings. Although these photographs work, they are not going to help you stand apart from everyone else that is selling products just like yours. In order to really stand out, you are going to want to use the sample products you received to take your pictures for Amazon.

There are a few key approaches that you can use to help you get a high-quality photograph for your listing. The first one is to remember that all of the best pictures follow a minimalist approach, as this supports your viewers with knowing exactly what you are selling. If you have too much going on in your picture, it can look overwhelming and draw eyes away, or it can cause people to wonder what exactly they are going to be purchasing from you.

STRIVE TO BE AN AMAZON FEATURED MERCHANT

This is an honor of the highest kind on Amazon for a seller. Your statistics, the feedback you receive, and your sales have to set a gold standard for other sellers. Amazon doesn't offer the title easily. As there have been very few merchants who have been awarded this, having a good seller profile won't cut it. Being a Featured Merchant can be achieved in a few months, and if your service is dedicated and well accomplished, the benefits are highly rewarding.

A Featured Merchant on Amazon is eligible to win the "Buy Box" service. The Buy Box service is very powerful, especially when your business sells several products across different categories. An integral component of the Amazon platform is that multiple sellers are providing the same product. Being an Amazon Featured Merchant and winning the Buy Box feature will give you default sales for the product.

USE THE RIGHT FULFILLMENT SERVICE

Amazon's FBA service offers several advantages for multiple audiences and is the obvious choice for the fulfillment services out there.

Review and follow Amazon's rules and guidelines.

FLEXIBILITY WITH PRICING STRATEGY AND PROMOTIONS

Putting your products on sale may occur, but sellers ensure that it is done to get a little more sales rank. Other reasons than that may not be beneficial to you. If you tend to lower your price just to be able to compete with others, then, it would not help your business. It is rather preferable to play with little competition.

DECIDE ON YOUR MARGINS

Successful sellers are those running the business to generate income and not to cost them money. Determining what your margin is needs careful decision together with identifying every fee involved.

LOOK OUT FOR MARKETING OPPORTUNITIES WITHIN AMAZON

Amazon is often offering different marketing opportunities to make an easy selling on Amazon. Taking advantage of it and using the tools provided by Amazon would open up new strategies for the business.

TAKE ADVANTAGE OF THE HOLIDAYS

One of the greatest times of the year for businesses is during holidays when sales possibly increase up to five times the average sales. And so, sellers are getting ready for these periods with a handful of inventories. Successful sellers are able to forecast the demand for their product so not to have excessive inventory by the time that the occasion has passed.

HANDLE YOUR PACKAGE AND LABEL WITH CARE

This is the part of the business that shouldn't be missed out. The products must be shipped to Amazon successfully. This means to provide proper and enough packing in shipping products to Amazon. Basically, it will ensure that your products won't be damaged, even when products are accidentally dropped.

USE THE AMAZON SELLER CENTRAL REPORTS

Inventory and sales reports are necessary for running a selling business. The good thing about being an Amazon seller is that there are reports available when you access your Amazon seller account. Make use of these reports in evaluating your business and how to improve it.

USE THE "PERFECT" FULFILLMENT SERVICE

The best-kept secret of Amazon sellers is using the Amazon FBA that provides the fulfillment service. It only takes a few bulk shipments to Amazon as compared to individually shipping orders to your customers. It simply frees up your time.

BE PROACTIVE IN MANAGING INVENTORY

Maintaining a healthy inventory on Amazon can make a good sales rank of your products. Amazon Sales Ranks are based on the quantity of the sale at a particular time. Consequently, non-stock affects the sales rank of your product because each day that your product makes no sale, the sales rank drops.

GIVE FEEDBACK ON CUSTOMER INQUIRIES IMMEDIATELY

Whenever a customer has questions, Amazon expects the seller to respond to customer questions within 24 hours. If you don't want to get a demerit on your account, you'd better answer customer communications quickly. To do this, log on your Seller Central page and set up the automation to receive customer questions on your email so you can also answer inquiries whenever you're not logged on Amazon.

CHECK THE UPC CODES WHEN LISTING PRODUCTS THOROUGHLY

Make sure to double check and read the full description and specs of the products before listing to Amazon carefully. You must be aware that there are manufacturers who do not change UPC codes whenever they make changes on the features of a product. When this happens and the item you sell is not the latest version of the product, expect returns with bad feedback from your buyers because of inappropriate items.

PREPARE ACCURATE PRODUCT DESCRIPTIONS

The product description is normally the customer's basis of buying decisions. The customer will notice even a slight difference between the description and the actual item when delivered. Describing a product accurately is what successful sellers practically do so that it won't lead to possible returns or negative feedbacks.

GET MORE FEEDBACK AND PRODUCT REVIEWS

Expect that Amazon buyers do not leave feedback naturally after purchasing a product. And usually, customers are more motivated to give feedback when they have a bad experience with the product. What sellers normally do is to ask customers to make a review or feedback because one of the most effective ways to market a product is having more feedback.

FOLLOW AMAZON IMAGE GUIDELINES

Buyers are enticed to buy a product usually through the product images shown. Product images help describe the items you are selling and provide a useful information to customers.

Currently, all photos are scaled to 500 x 500 pixels and photos that do not have a 1:1 dimension ratio are padded with white space on the shorter sides.

LABEL ITEMS AND SHIPMENTS CORRECTLY

There will always be an instance that you'll mislabel an item when you prepare for shipment to the fulfillment center, especially if you're not able to establish a process to double check each product and box. As your inventory increases, the possibility of mixing up labels may increase as well. And so, make sure to double check labeling so it won't mess up your shipments, reach your customer, and get a negative feedback from the buyer. In packing your product, it is also recommended that you can see the item inside the package as a way to double check the items when you box them to ship.

PACK SHIPMENTS TO AMAZON CORRECTLY

Give an extra effort to pack shipments meticulously to avoid delays and penalty fees. Amazon's packaging and shipping requirements are strictly followed when sending items to fulfillment centers. It ensures that items will not be damaged, be processed and fulfilled efficiently.

ACT ON NEGATIVE FEEDBACKS

Neutral or negative feedbacks on your products can automatically lose your featured seller status. If it falls below 95%, Amazon may cancel your account. Sellers take action to remove negative feedbacks through reaching out to the customers. What you can do is to immediately email the customer to extend your sincerest apology on what they have experienced from your product. Along with the apology could be an Amazon gift card as a token of sincerity, a $10 gift card is advisable.

Usually, the customer sends back to extend gratitude to you and that is the best time to explain how the error occurred, then, you can request to remove the feedback.

This won't guarantee a 100% positive response from the customers, but surely you can get over half of your negative feedbacks.

INCREASE SALES THROUGH BUY BOX

This is the page that is shown whenever a buyer clicks on one of the results that buyer searched on. The majority of the sales are earned through the "buy box" which is why sellers work on winning the buy box.

NEGOTIATE SELLING EXCLUSIVITY WITH SUPPLIERS

It is possible that a seller can be an exclusive seller of a particular manufacturer or supplier. Sellers usually scout for manufacturers in wholesale trade shows to negotiate selling exclusivity to Amazon since in most instances' owners are available in the booth.

USE THE AMAZON KEYWORDS WISELY

For any online business, keywords can make money for someone who knows how to use it. These are words or phrases that are typed in by Amazon buyers in the search box when they find products. It is good that Amazon provides a keyword field when sellers create a listing. You should learn how to use the keyword field that Amazon provides.

USE AMAZON FBA TO FULFILL MULTI-CHANNEL ORDERS

It is a good step to fulfill multi-channel orders using Amazon FBA if you sell your products or plan to sell to other channels like eBay or Etsy. Shipping charge may be less than UPS or Priority mail. You can create Fulfillment Order where you can fill in the buyer information. If later you want to automate fulfilling multi-channel orders, you may use. It is a service that connects your marketplace listing to FBA that automatically process when an item sells on eBay, sync inventory and get the item from the FBA inventory. This tool spares you from manual order entry and ship tracking.

SELECT THE RIGHT PRODUCT

Select products according to your storage space. When you're dealing with larger components like furniture and mattresses, you have to move out of your basement for storage. If there is an alternative warehouse you can use, then it won't be a problem. If you do not have a warehouse or storage unit, you should probably consider shifting to another product, one of smaller size.

BE FLEXIBLE

Pick a strategy and stick to it. Within certain conditions, a seller must adapt and act according to what is required at any particular time. If you are down on sales count, you can place an item for sale with a discount. Similarly, if you want to earn profits, look toward raising your prices on certain products that are in demand. The increment or decrement can be just a slight amount, but it could have a big influence on your income.

KNOW YOUR MARGIN

This is of great importance to any seller, as the margins are set to determine the sales. When you buy a product to sell, pricing the product low just for the sake of getting sales numbers is of no benefit. Indeed, it causes more harm to the business than good. Your pricing is crucial and can mean your product sales are producing a regrettable profit margin. The smaller the profit margin, the more your money is lost in taxes and miscellaneous charges. The ultimate payout drops to a point where the business is no longer functional as you run into debt. Keep track of those margins (through Excel spreadsheets or documents), as a better profit margin could lead your business to the point of independence. In other words, the numbers speak for themselves.

UTILIZE SELLER CENTRAL REPORTS

Amazon's website has a section known as "Seller Central," where you can access and update your seller account details. It is very popular in the seller community, as it offers tools and feedback reports. As a seller, it is important to analyze your numbers. These provide information regarding your sales, your feedback, your product promotions, your inventory details and your customer feedback (e.g., the reasons for refunds and returns). Download these reports and utilize them to create your seasonal demand chart. It won't be rewarding if you don't have enough stock of products that are favorites among the customers.

ENGAGE WITH REVIEWERS WHEN NECESSARY

Although Amazon is going to handle most of your customer care inquiries, it does not hurt to engage with some of them on your own as well. You can engage with reviewers easily by simply going onto your page, identifying what people are saying about your products, and writing back. Do not be afraid to leave comments like "thank you for your review!" under the comments that are positive and that are encouraging other people to purchase your products. If you find that people are leaving low-quality reviews, avoid getting defensive. Instead, ask them what they would like to see more of and how the experience could have been better. If it was something you can fix on your own, such as by finding a new supplier or making adjustments to your products or listings, do that. If it was something that needed to be managed by Amazon, ensure that your product reviewer has the right information to get in touch with Amazon so that they can receive support and have a more positive experience.

Although you do not have to do this, taking the time to engage on your own is going to help you have a more personal and positive impact in your business. You are also going to have the unique opportunity to see where you can improve on your service so that everyone has a positive experience with your shop. Through your own reviews, you can learn more about what new customizations and variations should be considered, what other products you can share, and how you can continue offering great quality. Never overlook the value of spending time reading your own reviews for support in growing your business on Amazon FBA.

OPTIMIZING YOUR PAGE FOR MOBILE VIEWING

Mobile phones these days are designed for us to have information in the palm of our hands and on the go. Any content you create today must be optimized for mobile viewing first and desktop second. This includes your Amazon FBA store (and other eCommerce stores you have). Customers are more likely to view your newsletters, product updates, emails, statutes, and tweets via mobile than on their desktop, and if your store is not optimized for mobile viewing, you are already on the losing end.

OPTIMAL PRICING IS A MUST

Every customer who goes to Amazon to purchase something often wants to buy products at the lowest price. No exceptions here. If you can get what you needed for a much lower cost, of course you would want to. As a seller, you need to think like your customer. You need to know the kind of prices that you will be competing against, and how to sell your products at the most optimal, competitive pricing. Items that are priced lower show up higher on the search results but be careful that it is not too low. Your pricing needs to be competitive and to do that, you can use Amazon's Match Low Price feature to assist you in consistently matching with the lowest pricing of the same product on Amazon.

YOU NEED THE BUY BOX

The Amazon Buy Box is the Holy Grail sellers strive to achieve. Located on the product detail page where customers start the purchasing process by adding items directly into their shopping cart, products listed here often see an increase in purchases.

ALWAYS IMPROVE, NEVER SLACK

Remember how you need to keep the same performance and standard going? Even when you have achieved steady success on Amazon? Using Amazon FBA means your packaging, shipping, and even customer service are handled by Amazon, but it does not mean you do not get to do anything else. Your job is to make sure your store is continuously selling and to do this, you need to consistently improve your store's performance and monitor it regularly. You need to be mindful of the sales, the seller rating as well as the return rates. You got your store to the top of its game, now you need to help it stay there.

NEVER NEGLECT THE REVIEWS

The best way for any customer to know that the products that they are purchasing are good value is by reading the reviews. Customers will click on products that have higher ratings and the likelihood of them finalizing purchases increases if products have good reviews and high ratings. Never give in to the temptation to cheat on your reviews. If you have a product that always gets bad, reviews-trash it. When you do, let your customers know that you are discontinuing it because this will help increase their confidence in your site. The fact that you have heard them and you are doing something about it increases brand trust.

FOLLOWING AMAZON'S RULES

Success does not come by cutting corners. Even if you do by some luck, you are not going to stay there for long. You can take advantage of tools and apps that help you be more efficient and up to date. Nevertheless, the golden rule here is to follow the rules set by Amazon and your account will not be penalized or suspended.

DETAILED IMAGE VIEW

You want to entice customers to purchase your products. Apart from a single photo, give users views from different angles as it can show character and carry a brand. Provide thoughtful and visually appealing imagery, and do not just show your products from one angle either. Always have a few different angles and views, with some zooming in on the finer details. Images are also a way your customer gathers information. If they love what they see, they will buy it. Purchasing stock photos is not as effective these days. Customers want to see the real deal where possible. If you are running your own eCommerce store, genuine pictures highlighting the lifestyle of your company, your employees, the surrounding of your firm is a hundred times better than regular stock photos.

SYSTEM INTEGRATION FOR EFFICIENCY

Integration allows you to synchronize various data such as orders, inventory, customers, items as well as shipping and tracking information between your other systems and Amazon. If you are on other channels, make it a point to integrate your sales channels with your backend systems. You can automate these processes and eliminate manual data entry, which can cause delayed data processing time as well as errors that are costly.

CONCLUSION

Amazon FBA can be a great place to start an online eCommerce business or an excellent addition to your already existing retail business. Novice sellers get to learn what it takes to run an online store without having to bear the burden of a massive risk that might land them in debt. The Amazon team is there to help you every step of the way, from the payments to the packaging, shipping and even dealing with your customer service, which is why it is the perfect passive income option. Minimal work on your part, but still good enough to generate a recurring income, even when you are not actively working on it yourself.

Many sellers have already found success on Amazon by either increasing their sales or boosting the visibility of their existing stores by branching out into Amazon FBA. You could be one of those sellers too.

Working with Amazon is like working with millions of sellers at the same time. Given the restricted categories of sales with Amazon, you will find a swarm of sellers selling the same commodities as you do. But you would have read the tactics given in Amazon FBA: The Complete Guide to Start Your Amazon FBA Business to stay ahead of competition. You will get to know about many more such things when you start working with Amazon FBA program of the company.

Being persistent with selling is the key to make success in this field. Like many other careers, Amazon FBA requires you to be determined and find ways to make maximum profit. But you must have figured out that it is not very complicated as it seemed to you earlier. You just need to spare a few hours every day or every week and stick to your routine.

I would not recommend that you quit everything and start dreaming of becoming wealthy with Amazon FBA. Give it a few hours in a week and then think about working on it full time if you can sustain with investments.

Now that you know the basics of Amazon FBA, go ahead with beginning the program and explore it inside out. Make the most of Seller Central and your Seller account and no one can stop you from making a fortune!

The next step is to stop reading and to start doing whatever is required of you in order to ensure that yourself and those you care about will be on good financial grounds and stability. If you find that you still need help getting started you will likely have better results by creating a schedule that you hope to follow including personal milestones and practical applications for various parts of the tasks as well as the overall process of acquiring the life changing knowledge and experiences.

Once you have finished the initial process it is important to understand that it is just that, only part of a larger plan of preparation. Your best chances for overall success will come by taking the time to learn as many vital skills as possible. Only by using your prepared status as a springboard to greater profit margins will you be able to truly rest soundly knowing that you are finally taking the right steps into realizing your financial balance and stability, not to mention prosperity.

How'd You Enjoy Reading *How to Sell on Amazon for Beginners*?

I want to say thank you for purchasing and reading this book! I hope you enjoyed it and it's provided value to your life. If you enjoyed reading this book and found some benefit in it, I'd love your support and hope that you could take a moment to post a review on Amazon. I'd love to hear from you, even if you have feedback, as it'll help me in ensuring that I improve this book and others in the future.

To leave your Amazon review, I've made it as easy as possible for you. Just click this link below or scan the QR code:

Click Here to Leave Your Amazon Review

I want to let you know that your review is very important to me and will help this book reach and impact more people's lives. Thanks for your time and support!